Embroidery

by Diana Springall

with contributions by Jan Beaney, Sue Rangely, Julia Caprara and Jackie Hill

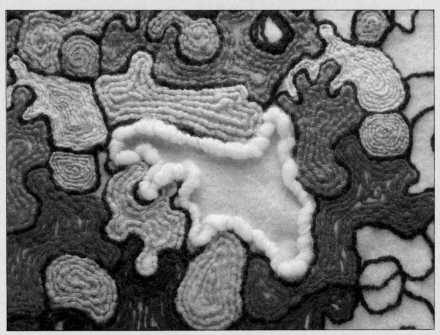

Edited by Jenny Rogers

British Broadcasting Corporation

This book accompanies the BBC Television series *Embroidery*
first broadcast from September 1980. Producer : Jenny Rogers

The book may be used independently of the broadcasts

Published to accompany a series of
programmes in consultation with the
BBC Continuing Education Advisory Council

© Diana Springall, Jan Beaney and the
British Broadcasting Corporation 1980
First published 1980
Published by the British Broadcasting
Corporation, 35 Marylebone High Street,
London W1M 4AA   ISBN 0 563 16385 2

This book is set in 10/11 Monophoto Photina
by Tradespools Ltd, Frome, Somerset
Printed in Wales by Severn Valley
Press Ltd, Caerphilly, Mid Glamorgan

Contents

Designers

Diana Springall items on pages 11,
20, 26, 29, 30, 31, 34, 36, 41, 43,
44, 50, 52, 57, 61, 74, 75.
Jan Beaney pages 15, 16, 17, 18, 19,
38, 47, 54, 63, 64, 78.
Sue Rangely pages 66, 69.
Julia Caprara pages 58, 59.
Jackie Hill page 72.

Photography and illustration

Photographs: Bob Komar
Diagrams: Hayward and Martin Ltd

Introduction

This book aims to introduce you to the delights of modern embroidery. It is for anyone with an interest in fabric, thread, colour and texture. It assumes that you have no special knowledge of embroidery and its techniques, though perhaps you may already have made up a canvas work kit or a transfer-printed linen with stranded cotton.

We have chosen a core of techniques which seem to offer special interest to the embroiderer. Around these techniques we have designed many projects: bags, belts, pictures, shirts, bedcovers, a mirror frame, cushions, rugs, pincushions, a lampshade and so on. These are only intended as beginnings: you will be able to think of many more variants. In most cases we have done the major part of the designing for you and given instructions, but many projects leave considerable scope for individual development. Some projects are quick, small scale and simply made. Some are more demanding and will need weeks of consistent dedication. Embroidery has a long and very honourable history in most parts of the world. Techniques arrived at in the past are so diverse that it would be almost impossible to invent new ones. However in the last twenty years there has been one striking development: embroidery has now become an art form in its own right.

For instance, it is studied at degree level in art colleges by people who previously might have become painters or sculptors. At the same time the old, highly skilled craft techniques have been continued. Craftsmanship, once considered an end in itself, must now share the limelight with original design. It is no longer good enough just to go on repeating the glories of the past: each embroiderer must now make his or her own design decisions too. This is not intended to be a fully comprehensive embroidery book: there are many such books already available. Rather, it is intended to start you, very selectively and gently on the road to designing for yourself. Thinking for yourself, on however humble a level, adds enormously to any craft, but to embroidery it adds fulfilment unsurpassed.

Metric and imperial measurements have been given throughout (except for fabric lengths which are now almost universally sold by the metre only). These are not always exact equivalents, so it would be better to stick to one or the other.

We have given precise quantities, colours and sizes where appropriate. In some projects, however, the degree of individual choice is so wide that this has not been possible and we must leave you to work out quantities according to the effect you

want to achieve. In some cases where quantities are small, we have left out measurements on the assumption that you may already have spare pieces of yarn, fabric or canvas that you could use up.

Abbreviations used in this book	
RS	Right side
WS	Wrong side

Imperial and metric equivalents	
$\frac{1}{8}$ in	3 mm
$\frac{1}{4}$ in	5 mm
$\frac{1}{2}$ in	1 cm
$\frac{5}{8}$ in	1.5 cm
$\frac{3}{4}$ in	2 cm
1 in	2.5 cm
$1\frac{1}{2}$ in	4 cm
$1\frac{3}{4}$ in	4.5 cm
2 in	5 cm
$2\frac{1}{2}$ in	6 cm
3 in	7.5 cm
4 in	10 cm
5 in	13 cm
6 in	15 cm
7 in	18 cm
8 in	20.5 cm
9 in	23 cm
10 in	25.5 cm
11 in	28 cm
12 in	30.5 cm
$\frac{1}{2}$ yd	45.5 cm
1 yd	91.5 cm
2 yd	1.90 m
3 yd	2.80 m
4 yd	3.70 m

Equipment

One of the most satisfying features of embroidery as a craft is that you need so little in the way of specialised or expensive equipment.

SCISSORS

Small embroidery scissors
These have long, fine points for cutting and trimming threads and small shapes.

Cutting-out shears or dressmaking scissors
Buy the longest blades you can find. Choose a pair with large finger holes which will take all four fingers of your hand comfortably.

Paper scissors
Keep a pair of medium sized scissors specially for this job. Cutting paper gradually blunts the blades – this will spoil them for cutting cloth.

NEEDLES

From left to right, below

Tapestry
These have a large, long eye which can carry a thick thread without distorting the canvas. The needle has a blunt point which protects the threads from damage.

Crewel
This is the most commonly used embroidery needle, a smaller version of the chenille and for use with finer cloth and threads.

Beading needle
This is a fine, long, sharp needle specially designed to pass through very small beads.

Sharps
This is necessary for all fine sewing. Essential for assembling fabrics and particularly useful for carrying sewing cotton.

Chenille
This is exactly like a tapestry needle but with a sharp point. It is designed to carry a thick thread through cloth without piercing too large a hole.

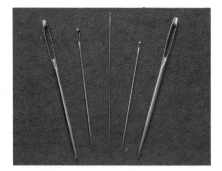

FRAMES

It is perfectly possible to work a lot of embroidery without a frame. Some people prefer to hold the work in their hands and to give more time to carefully stretching it afterwards. However, once you become used to working with a frame it is faster and produces less distortion of 'grain' than hand-held work. For large scale work simply make a large frame.

Hoop or tambour frames
These simple, circular frames are essential items for all free machine embroidery. They are also a great help in achieving the perfect technique in many surface stitches. They are mostly used with soft material which will not be damaged by ring marks. A 20 cm (8 in) frame is a good all-purpose size.

Rectangular frames
These need only be four pieces of wood carefully measured and then securely joined together with simple screw-on flat angle brackets bought from chain stores or ironmongers. If you are a more skilled carpenter, then you could secure the joints by pinning or glueing. If you find that carpentry of any kind at all is too demanding, then an old picture frame will do. It is perfectly adequate for forms of embroidery like canvas work where the background cloth is stiff and should not be subjected to harsh ring marks which a tambour frame would leave. The frame will also help keep the canvas taut, preserving its true grain.
It is not usually necessary to buy an expensive adjustable frame except for gold work.

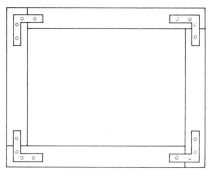

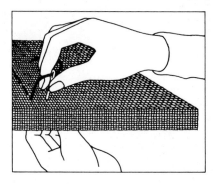

Using the frame
One hand should always be above the frame and one always beneath. Use alternate pushing and pulling movements, stabbing the needle up and down. This movement becomes smooth and easy with practice.

OTHER USEFUL EQUIPMENT

Pins
Use dressmaker's steel pins. A box lined with black paper will help keep them rust-free.

Stapler
One of these is invaluable for attaching work to frames. An office stapler which opens out will do, but a staple 'gun' (much quicker to use) will be a useful investment for a really productive embroiderer.

Stiletto
These are for piercing holes in cloth before making eyelets and for easing thick threads through fabric.

Non-woven interfacing
Vilene has widespread uses, for instance, in appliqué or for backing some types of patchwork. It comes in several different weights to match the weight of fabric it is to support. There are two types: iron-on and sew-in. It can be bought by the metre from fabric departments.

Paper-backed adhesive
This is also useful, for instance, for appliqué. It is ironed on to fabric and the paper is then peeled away. Next time it is pressed it will melt and stick, so it must then be between two layers of fabric to be stuck together.

Fabric adhesives
Adhesives in liquid form are essential for some types of appliqué and also for assembling and finishing other work. The ideal one is a rubber solution which will leave no marks even if it is accidentally spilt on the right side of the fabric.

Stanley knife
This is a craft knife with heavy-duty blades, for cutting mounting-board.

Metal rule

It is advisable to use a long metal ruler or a wooden one with a metal edge when cutting mounting board.

Masking tape

This is for binding the raw edges of canvas to prevent them unravelling during working. A wide, heavy-duty tape with a fabric-like surface on one side, sticky on the other, is ideal.

DESIGN EQUIPMENT

No 1 paintbrush
and white poster paint

These are used for transferring the designs on to cloth.

French chalk

This is also used to transfer designs, see the 'prick and pounce' method on the next page.

Tailor's chalk or white pencil

These are used for drawing lines and patterns on cloth.

Pencil

An HB pencil is the best sort for general drawing and tracing.

Fine felt-tip or ball-point pen

This is used for drawing on canvas or for making lines dark enough to show through tracing paper. Make sure it is waterproof if you use it on canvas, or it may run during the stretching process (see page 8).

Tracing paper

Buy proper, stout tracing paper from an art supplier or stationer. Kitchen greaseproof paper is not usually transparent or strong enough.

Cartridge paper

This is the most versatile paper for drawing and it is useful for making paper templates.

THREADS

All sorts of threads can be used from string, ribbon and raffia, to the finest gold and silver threads. Enthusiastic embroiderers will collect any interesting-looking oddment they see, and store it away carefully for some possible future use. There are now many firms which will supply both standard and specialised ranges by mail order. The first five threads described below appear from left to right in the photograph above.

Stranded cotton

This is made up of six fine, lustrous, soft threads which can be parted and used singly or in any combination. There is a very wide colour range.

Perlé

This is a non-stranded cotton thread with a pearly finish.

Tapestry wool

A soft yarn, commonly selected for canvas work although it is not particularly hard wearing. It is sometimes called *Laine Tapisserie*.

Carpet thrums

These are the odd lengths of wool left over from carpet manufacture. It is a beautiful thread – firm, twisted and exceptionally hard wearing but the colours and dye-lots are rather unpredictable. This is available by

mail order or direct from mills and factories in carpet making areas.

Turkey rug wool

This is thick and hard wearing with a fairly rough texture. It is useful on large canvas or on very open-weave fabrics. *Laine à broder* is an equally thick rug wool, but much softer and lighter in weight.

Crewel wool

This is also used for canvas work, but it is harder wearing and has an attractive twist to the ply.

Weaving yarns

These are available from specialist shops and by mail order. They are generally firm and textured in a variety of thicknesses.

Knitting yarns

These change with fashion, but there is usually a wide range available: smooth and textured, fine and thick. Knitting yarn generally has a more stretchy, elastic character than the embroidery or weaving threads.

Sewing cotton

These are available in a variety of thicknesses and fibres. The general rule for assembly jobs is to match synthetic threads to synthetic fabrics, and natural threads to natural fabrics, because synthetic threads have more 'stretch' than natural ones. *Machine embroidery cotton* is finer and softer than sewing cotton and therefore gives a more delicate effect. *Silk threads* and *Buttonhole twist* can also be useful for stitchery projects.

How to enlarge a design

This is a useful technique. Some embroidery designs in magazines (and a few in this book) are shown smaller than they should be worked, because of restrictions in page size. Also, when you begin designing for yourself, it may be necessary to draw the design much smaller than the size you will want to embroider. Alternatively, you may see a small drawing or photograph which you want to trace and then enlarge.

MATERIALS

Strong tracing paper to cover the original drawing

Cartridge paper slightly bigger than the finished size you need

Ruler

Pencil

Rubber

Fine felt-tip or ball-point pen

METHOD

1 Trace the design on to the tracing paper using the pencil.
2 Draw a rectangle around the traced design and then divide it into equal squares. A simple design could be divided into 2.5 cm (1 in) squares, a more intricate one may need smaller squares. Number and letter each square down and across. (See the diagram below.)
3 Take your piece of cartridge paper and secure the tracing to it in the bottom left-hand corner.
4 Next, draw in the diagonal (cb) and extend it on to the cartridge paper, right to its edge.
5 Decide how wide you want the finished work to be, then extend the bottom line of the rectangle (cd) across on to the cartridge paper to that width. From that point, draw a line upwards to meet the long diagonal line. It is important that this line is perfectly upright so that the corners of the design rectangle are right angles.
6 Measure the height of the vertical line and extend ca on to the cartridge paper to exactly the same height. From this point draw a horizontal line across to complete the enlarged rectangle.
7 Remove the tracing paper and draw in the bottom left hand corner of the rectangle.
8 Count the squares in the small tracing paper rectangle and divide the large rectangle into the same number. Number and letter them in exactly the same way, so that you can refer quickly to each square.
9 Now carefully copy the lines of the traced design from the small squares to the large ones. Do this in pencil so that you can easily rub out mistakes. The same 'squaring' method can be adapted if you want to reduce a large design.

Transferring designs: 1 Template method

This is suitable for transferring a very simple shape or one that is to be repeated several times.
1 First trace the shape on to good quality tracing paper and cut it out.
2 Pin the paper shape to the fabric, then using small stitches, tack all round the shape close to its edge. Use a thread which contrasts with the colour of the material.
3 Remove the paper.
Alternatively, a shape can be cut out in thin card and drawn around with tailor's chalk. Tack along the line (the chalk alone would wear away while you are working).
The most suitable method will vary with the project. Whichever you use, it is normally best to transfer the design before it is put in the frame for working.

2 Prick and pounce

This method is best for transferring an intricate design.

MATERIALS

Tracing paper

A small square of felt, bunched up to make a pad

Crewel needle

No 1 paint brush

Poster paint matching fabric colour

French chalk or talcum powder

HB pencil

METHOD

1 Trace the design on to strong tracing paper.
2 Pick up the piece of tracing paper and with the crewel needle poke holes from the *underside* of the drawing through to the RS, about 5 mm ($\frac{1}{4}$ in) apart. This will leave smooth holes on the underside, and rough holes with a 'cheesegrater' appearance on the upper side.
3 Lay the tracing on to the fabric with the rough holes uppermost, smooth holes against the fabric. Line it up carefully and secure with pins.
4 With your small pad of felt, dip into the french chalk and rub it gently through the holes. Remove

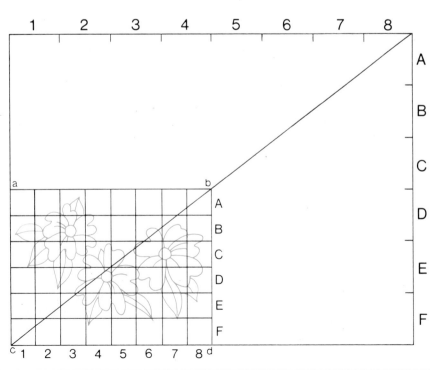

the tracing paper. There will now be small powder dots on the fabric. Repeat the process if it is an all-over design to cover a large area.

5 Using the fine brush and paint, carefully join up all the dots to form the outline of the design which will be embroidered.

3 Direct tracing

A simple canvas work design can always be traced direct by laying the canvas over the design as long as the original has first been darkened sufficiently. Line it up carefully and copy with a *waterproof* felt-tip pen.

Finishing work: stretching

When you have put many hours of work into an embroidery, it is well worth spending a little more time to finish it well.

Stretching is essential to achieve a good finish. It will remove the crinkles and distortions which can creep in while work is in progress. Pressing may *very occasionally* be an appropriate method of finishing, but it is usually not advisable as it will flatten the threads.

MATERIALS

Drawing board or wooden surface

Several layers of blotting paper

Drawing pins

METHOD

1 Lay several layers of blotting paper on a drawing board or an old wooden surface.

2 Thoroughly wet the blotting paper with water.

3 Lay the work on it *face upwards* as in the diagram below.

4 Starting at the centre top, insert drawing pins along the top edge, making sure the fabric grain is straight.

5 Pull the opposite side of the work hard and then insert pins at close intervals all along the bottom edge, keeping the work taut.

6 Treat the other edges in the same way, continuing to add pins until there are no wrinkles left.

7 Allow to dry in a warm place overnight before removing pins.

Mounting work: 1 Panels

These are embroideries which are held on to a firm base. There are two ways of doing it, but the work must be stretched first in both cases, by following the method above.

The first method is suitable for embroideries less than 36 cm (14 in) in height or width.

You will need strong cardboard or mounting board, cut carefully to the exact size of the finished panel.

You should allow turnings of at least 4 cm (1½ in) around the edges of the embroidery. If these edges are likely to fray, you should zig-zag them first. Place the embroidery RS down on a flat surface and position the board carefully over it. Thread a darning or carpet needle with fine string or carpet twine and knot it at the end. Fold over the top and the bottom turnings, and beginning at their centres, lace them together working outwards. Keep turning the work over to check that it is really taut. Bring the side turnings over, and lace these together in the same way, folding the corners in as neatly as possible (see diagram, right).

The second method is suitable for larger embroideries.

Make or buy a simple, firm, wooden frame using the same method as for

making a frame to work on (see page 5). Lay the embroidery RS down on a flat surface and position the frame carefully over it.

Starting at the centre of the top and bottom turnings, gently pull the embroidery into place and secure it with drawing pins. Do the same at the two centre sides. Turn the frame over, and check the position of the work on the RS. If all is well, replace the drawing pins with staples and continue stapling all the way round, pulling gently to keep the work taut. The back can be neatened by adding a felt or fabric lining which is slip-stitched to the embroidery. If you want a frame to show from the RS, this is better done by professionals, unless you are a skilled carpenter. Professional framing will cost less if you have already mounted the embroidery yourself.

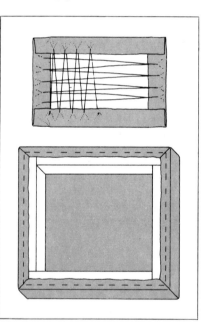

Note Modern embroidery is probably better left unglazed as the glass can spoil the textural effects – it puts a barrier between the embroidery and the onlooker! Dust can usually be adequately removed with a feather duster. However, some people feel happier if a precious embroidery is protected by glass. In this case, you could stretch and mount if yourself before taking it for professional framing and glazing.

2 Hangings

This method is best for making up embroideries which need to drape softly for their full effect.

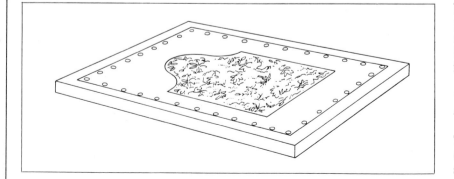

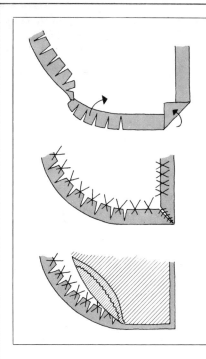

Stretch or press the embroidery. Cut an interlining (e.g. Non-woven interfacing) to the size of the finished work.

Gently bring all the raw edges over the interlining and pin. Where there are curves, snip. Carefully stitch all these turnings into the interfacing with herringbone. Be careful not to catch any of the front material. Now cut a lining the size of the finished article, plus 1.5 cm ($\frac{5}{8}$ in) turnings all round.

Turn raw edges all round. Tack and press. Slip stitch invisibly to the embroidery.

Making-up cushions

Remove the embroidery from the frame. Then stretch or press as appropriate and trim to within 1.5 cm ($\frac{5}{8}$ in) all round.

Cut a piece of material exactly the same size for the back of the cushion. Place two RS together. Tack and machine three of the sides. If the embroidered half is canvas work, be careful to stitch close to the last row of embroidery. Clip the corners to reduce the bulk. Neaten the two remaining raw edges by zigzag stitch or by overcasting by hand.

Press and turn to RS. Gently push out corners with a point turner or a pencil.

Insert the cushion pad, then close the opening with neat slip stitches.

Piped cushions

Buy the appropriate length of piping cord which comes in a variety of thicknesses. Cut and join some crossway strips of fabric about 4 cm (2 in) wide. Wrap the fabric RS outwards round cord. Put the zip foot attachment on the sewing machine to enable you to machine really close to the cord.

Take the embroidered front of the cushion and tack the piping to the RS, all raw edges together. Machine all round. On square or rectangular cushions, snip into corners almost up to the piping.

To join the piping, trim both ends of the cord so they just overlap. Unravel and cut away half the strands of each end, then twist the two ends together and secure with a few stitches. Join the fabric part of the piping with slip stitches. Place the embroidered front of cushion and material for the back RS together and finish as for plain cushion.

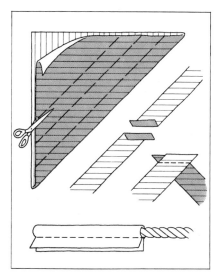

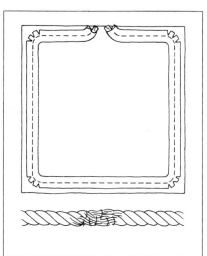

Twisted cords

These are useful in embroidery, and can be used to put around the seam of a plain cushion. They are quite easy to do, and can be made in any thickness. You will need a knitting needle, plenty of thread, a helper and a convenient door knob.

The distance between yourself and the doorknob should be about three times the length of the finished cord you need.

Wind the thread between the knob and the knitting needle several times (say four). Now begin rotating the needle, thus twisting the cord. Stop twisting when the yarn begins to go into bundles. Ask your helper to hold the centre of the cord while you bring up the knitting needle to the door handle and gently release the door knob end of the yarn. You are now holding both ends of the cord. The helper then lets go, and you give the cord a really fierce shake. It then twists itself into its final thickness. You can put a slip knot in the 'loose' end to hold it together while you are working.

Attach the cord to a cushion with tiny, invisible catch stitches, neatening and joining the raw ends.

Useful books

BEANEY, J. *Embroidery: new approaches* Pelham Books, 1978.
BUTLER, A. *The Batsford encyclopedia of embroidery stitches* Batsford, 1979.
CLABBURN, P. *The needleworker's dictionary* Macmillan, 1976.
COLBY, A. *Patchwork* Batsford, 1958; n.e. paperback 1976.
DENNE, L. de and JOHNSON, M. *Decorating with stitches* Bell and Hyman, 1978.
EDWARDS, J. *Crewel embroidery in England* Batsford, 1975.
HOWARD, C. *Inspiration for embroidery* Batsford, 1967.
JONES, N. *Embroidery* (Guidelines) Macdonald, 1979.
MCNEILL, M. *Quilting for today* Mills and Boon, 1976.
RISLEY, C. *Machine embroidery: a complete guide* Studio Vista, 1973; n.e. paperback, 1979.
SHORT, E. *Quilting: technique, design and application* Batsford, 1979.
SPRINGALL, D. *Canvas embroidery* Batsford, 1969 n.e. due April, 1980.
WHYTE, K. *Design in embroidery* Batsford, 1969.

Appliqué

If you are not a very experienced embroiderer, appliqué is an excellent way to start. It simply involves cutting shapes out in one fabric and applying them to a background fabric. Immediate colour effects are possible and you can plan out the whole design before actually stitching. One other benefit of the technique is that where pictures and panels are concerned you can mix fabrics of different weights.

Appliqué is versatile: it can be used to decorate clothes and house-hold linen, though here the fabrics must be all of the same weight and type to minimise washing and wearing problems. There are three basic techniques:
1 Using a swing needle (or zigzag stitch) machine to cover raw edges.
2 Covering the raw edge by hand with herringbone stitch.
3 'Blind' appliqué, where the edges are turned under and attached with slip stitches.
Appliqué can be very successfully padded, stuffed and quilted. It can also form a good basis for further embellishment with stitchery.

TO AVOID PUCKERING

Tack the pieces in position first, matching grains. This means putting the straight grain of the piece to be applied on the straight grain of the background fabric. On most fabrics the straight grain can be seen as vertical lines parallel to the selvedge.

Appliqué landscape picture

This simple landscape picture was inspired by a painting of Kent in spring. A wide variety of fabrics has been used: dress cottons, velvets and furnishing fabrics.

Our diagram of the picture is shown overleaf in a size that could be transposed as it is. However, it would not be difficult to enlarge by scaling it up proportionally (see page 7). You could also try finding a landscape picture in a magazine, or even sketching your own and using the appliqué technique described here.

MATERIALS

One piece background fabric 46 cm × 26 cm (18 in × 10 in)
Firm, iron-on interfacing the same size
A variety of fabrics for appliqué
Fine, felt-tip pen
Pure rubber solution for attaching small areas without sewn edges
Sewing cottons to match fabrics
Strong card for mounting

METHOD

1 Place the interfacing (sticky side facing you) over the book and trace off the drawing. Make sure each half of the drawing matches exactly.

2 Mark each shape with a vertical arrow (this will later match the direction of the straight grain on your applied fabrics).
3 Now cut out the first shape from the interfacing. Place it glistening side down on the wrong side of the fabric to be applied. The arrow on the interfacing must match the straight grain of the fabric. Iron to make the bond. The interfacing strengthens the fabric and helps prevent it fraying.
4 Cut out the fabric shape, cutting round the edge of the interfacing. Place it in position, WS of applied piece to RS of background fabric.
5 Tack all round with small stitches, but not too near the edge otherwise the tacking can become caught up in the machine stitches later.

6 Attach permanently by hand, or machine using zigzag stitch. Each machine has its own instruction manual, so refer to that first. Use only half the maximum width on a small panel like this, otherwise the stitching lines will be too heavy. Your aim should be to enclose the raw edge completely with stitching. The bond between applied pieces and background fabric must be strong enough to withstand the stretching process later.

Hand herringbone stitch is a useful alternative to machine zigzag. This stitch gives a firm attachment as well as curbing fraying satisfactorily. The diagram on the right shows the stitch, much enlarged.

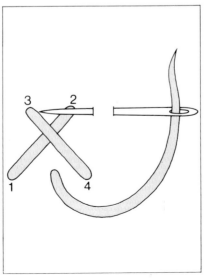

7 When you have planned, cut and sewn the basic shapes, cut a second range of the smaller shapes. These can be stuck on with rubber solution and embellished by hand stitchery.
8 Secure all loose ends of thread.
9 Stretch and mount (see page 8).

Denim pockets and bag to match

There are many jeans on the market each designed with a different shape pocket. Whichever shape they happen to be, it is possible to remove them, decorate them with a simple applied motif in additional denim, and return them to position. Using the same technique you could also make a small bag identical in shape and decoration.

MATERIALS

Scraps of denim

Cartridge paper for cutting out shapes

Sewing cotton

Firm, iron-on interfacing

METHOD

1 Carefully remove the pocket from the jeans.

2 Cut a paper shape identical to the shape of the pocket.

3 Boldly cut away a few shapes from the paper, making sure that the areas remaining are positive silhouettes. In our diagram below the dark areas would be cut away, leaving the light area to be used for the template.

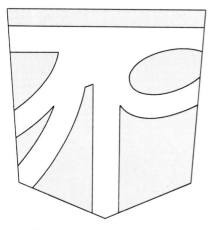

4 When you are satisfied with your design, iron on the interfacing to RS of an area of your denim scraps. *Note* you are using the light or WS for the decorative effect.

5 Place your paper pattern onto the denim piece and cut it out.

6 Lay your motif onto the RS of the pocket. Pin and tack.

7 Attach by herringbone stitch or machine zigzag.

8 A small bag can be made in a similar way but this time making two identical pocket shapes, using the jean pocket as a pattern and adding seam allowances all round. Place the two pieces RS together and close side seams. Turn to RS, hem the two top edges and then top stitch the side seams 1 cm ($\frac{1}{2}$ in) in from the turned edges.

9 Straps can either be made from narrow braid or from folding a strip of denim 2.5 cm (1 in) so that the raw edges meet in the middle and are overcast together, with a row of zigzag to cover the complete join.

Appliqué flower cushion

This cushion was inspired by the spring clematis 'Montana'. Using it as a guide, you could draw any simple flower shape for similar effects. The 'flowers' here are identical in shape, but each could be different if you wish. They are scattered in a cascade over the calico.

MATERIALS

50 cm unbleached calico

Scraps of dress cotton or poplin in a range of pale pinks and lilacs (the equivalent of 30 cm)

30 cm medium iron-on interfacing

One reel each of Gutterman buttonhole twist sewing thread in pale pink, rose pink, lilac and yellow

Cartridge paper

METHOD

1 Place the interfacing over the flower shape on the right and trace the shape directly on to it in one corner. Cut it out.
2 Place the shape on to the paper. Draw carefully round it and cut it out to use as a template.
3 Iron the interfacing on to the pink and lilac material. Use the template to draw flower shapes on the WS of the interfaced fabrics, then cut out as many as you need.
4 Arrange the shapes in a flowing. informal arrangement on the calico. Groups of flowers can contrast with more isolated ones.
5 Pin and tack carefully in position, then work zigzag stitch over all the raw edges.
6 Using the buttonhole twist in colours that match the flower shapes, embellish each outline with running stitch (see page 59) placed slightly away from the edge.
7 Make up the cushion (see page 9 for instructions).

Note the jug shape on the right is used for the kitchen blind, page 18.

Kitchen blind in calico and poplin

A simple repeat motif from a kitchen jug shape, forms the border of a blind measuring 86.5 cm (34 in) wide with a 120 cm (4 ft) drop. It is suitable for a standard 90 cm (3 ft) window.

MATERIALS

Roller blind kit

1.50 m unbleached calico

50 cm medium iron-on interfacing

50 cm orange poplin

Sewing cotton

Cartridge paper

METHOD

1 Trace the jug shape on page 16 on to the interfacing and using the template method described for the cushion on that page, cut out jug shapes from the orange material. *Note* you will need to reverse the template to get the jug's handles going in different directions. All jug shapes should be cut on the straight grain of the fabric.

2 Arrange jug shapes so that they almost touch, tack carefully, then work zigzag stitch over all raw edges.

3 To make up the blind, follow the kit instructions. The side hems on our blind have been turned once and machined, turned a second time and stuck with liquid fabric adhesive in order to save a line of machine stitches on the right side. The tab is a folded strip of calico which also has a machined finish.

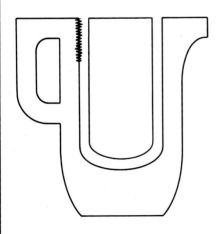

Little sweet pin cushion

The inspiration for this pin cushion came from looking at sweets.
Blind applique is used to attach the shapes, which also have a tiny
amount of 'trapunto' stuffing.

MATERIALS

Scraps of Thai silk or other kinds of 'shot' fabric

Scraps of iron-on interfacing if the chosen fabric frays badly

Sewing cottons in colours that match your fabrics

Scraps of stuffing material

Piping cord

Lengths of stranded cotton or silk buttonhole twist

METHOD

1 Cut out two square pieces of material to use as a backing fabric, 13 cm × 13 cm (5 in × 5 in).

2 Cut out four slightly rounded squares (not identical) for the first appliqué layer. If the chosen fabric frays badly, back it with iron-on interfacing at this stage. Turn under the raw edges and tack all round.

3 Cut out four slightly smaller shapes and treat in the same way. Attach these smaller shapes to the bigger shapes with tiny slip stitches all round.

Using buttonhole twist, outline the centre of each square with tiny back stitches in buttonhole twist or stranded cotton. Very carefully, using just the points of your embroidery scissors, snip an opening on the wrong side of each unit inside the back stitched square. Stuff. Quickly overcast the opening.

4 Attach the four units to the backing using slip stitches.

5 Following the instructions on page 9, cut a bias (crosswise) strip about 53 cm (21 in) long and make a piping with thin piping cord. Make up as for a cushion (see also page 9).

Elephant
in felt appliqué

This elephant was inspired by the beautiful traditional embroidered toy elephants of India. Felt is very suitable for appliqué as it never frays and has a wide range of colours. You can decorate the appliqué in any way you like: for instance, with gold threads, beads or tassles.

This is a demanding project suitable for a more experienced embroiderer.

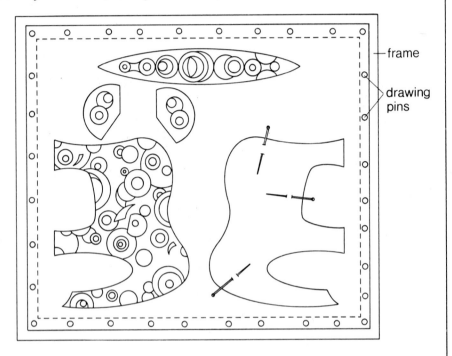

frame

drawing pins

MATERIALS

30 cm (12 in) of 90 cm (36 in) wide felt for chosen background colour *or* three 30 cm (12 in) felt squares

Scraps of felt in eight other colours

Sewing cottons in colours matching the felts to be applied (or one strand of stranded cotton can be used)

Sewing cotton to match the background felt, for making up

Bag (400 g) 100% polyester soft filling or best quality kapok

23 cm (9 in) lightweight sew-in interfacing

Oddments of string or piping cord

Imitation gold thread

Small embroidery scissors

No 9 sharp needle

Ball-point pen

Knitting needle, for stuffing

Rectangular frame

METHOD

1 First decide on a colour scheme. We have used nine colours including the basic beige for the ground colour.
2 Lay the interfacing over diagrams on pages 23 and 24. Using a fine ball-point pen, trace the elephant shapes and then the decorative circles: body (twice), ears (twice) and top gusset (once). These are the areas to be decorated.
3 Carefully cut out the shapes.
4 Lay these five interfacing shapes on to the ground colour and pin them to the felt. Using small stitches, carefully tack round the outside of each shape. Remove pins and take away interfacing. You now have the

outline shapes in tacking stitches on the felt.
5 Attach the felt to a frame with staples or drawing pins.
6 Now take one of the interfacing shapes, and using very sharp scissors cut one circle out of it to use as a template. Pin it to coloured felt and cut it out.
7 You can now decide whether you want the applied felt circles to be flat or raised by padding. Our elephant has a mixture of both, using several different techniques each of which gives a slightly different effect.
These are:
Felt padded with another layer of felt underneath. The underlayer is cut a fraction smaller than the upper one (diagram b).
Felt stuffed with cotton wool just before the final stitches (c).
Felt laid down over string which has been secured in place on the backing first (d).
Felt sewn on one edge only (e).

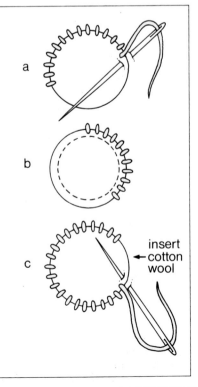

a

b

c

insert cotton wool

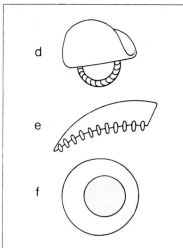

Felt cut away to reveal another colour underneath (f). All the shapes are applied in the same way with small overcast stitches (a).
8 Go on cutting out circles and applying them one at a time to the basic felt shape. There will be a few places where circles overlap and you will not be able to cut them from the interfacing shape. You will have to re-trace the top circle onto an extra piece of interfacing.
9 When the decoration is complete, remove the work from the frame and cut out on outline.
10 Now trace the remaining body shapes (the undecorated ones) on to the interfacing. Pin and cut out in felt: under-gusset (two), sole (four), tail (one).

To make up
All the stitching is done from the RS, with WS together throughout.
1 Stitch the under-gusset from A to opening and from B to opening, using double overcasting stitch (see diagram, right).
2 Place the gusset on the left main body section. Stitch from foot, E to B. Stitch from F to A.
Now complete the left side of the body by joining the undergusset in one seam from G to H.

3 Repeat these stages for the right hand side of the body.
4 Stitch up back seam from A to D. Check the pattern for the position of D. Join the back gusset from D along the back edge, over the head and down part of the trunk to C. Join the edge of trunk C to J. Finish the back head gusset section by sewing from C to D on the remaining side. Join the trunk B to K. The only open sections are now: under-gusset opening, feet and end of trunk. Attach soles and trunk end.

21

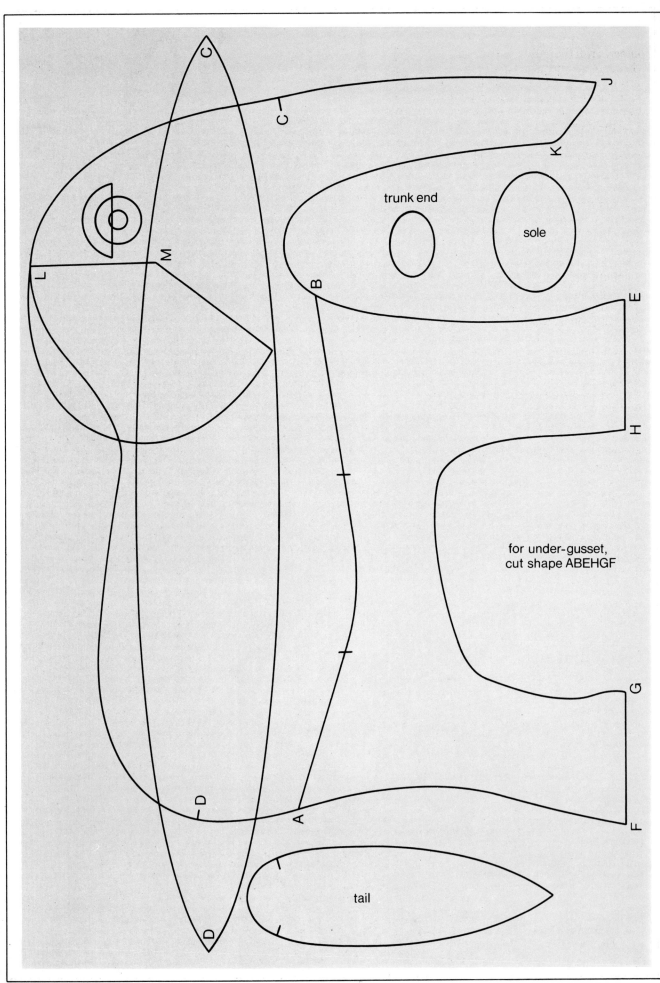

trunk end

sole

for under-gusset,
cut shape ABEHGF

tail

Stuffing

Using a knitting needle and fore-finger, push the filling into the body through the under-gusset opening, first towards the head, then the rest of the body section, taking a *small* amount of filling at a time. Push it into the tops of the legs and fill each leg firmly. Keep pushing with the needle until really firm. Now fill the trunk in the same way.

Finishing touches

1 Fold the tail piece on the centre line and stitch from point to top. Flatten the top end of the tail and stitch in place just above D. Then stitch the tail to the back seam for about an inch.

2 To make ears: trap a piece of cord or string between two layers of 'ear' and overcast the edges. Back stitch right up against the cord to hold it in place.
Join the ears to the body L to M.

3 Cut two eyelids and slash the lower edge to make eyelashes, then attach to the face.

4 Stitch up the opening in the gusset seam and add more filling if necessary.

5 Decorate with tassels, pom-pons or beads.

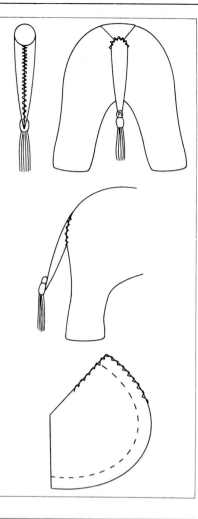

Canvas work

*Canvas work is embroidery on canvas, and is often described
as 'tapestry' (true tapestry is woven on a loom, so 'canvas work'
is a more correct name). In America it is called 'needlepoint'
but this is more correctly the name for needle-made lace.
It is a versatile, basic and useful embroidery technique with
a long history. It is exceptionally hard wearing, so was often
used in the past for upholstery and soft furnishing.
Alongside these practical items, there were 'representational'
pictures, usually done in tent or cross stitch. Both these
traditions continue to thrive today alongside the more
adventurous modern work. Canvas work is simple to do.
The canvas itself is evenly woven, so it lends itself to
geometric designs and is thus an ideal technique for people
beginning to design for themselves.*

CHOOSING A CANVAS

There are two basic types of canvas:
mono or single thread, penelope or
double-thread. Single weave is the
easiest to count and will take a far
greater variety of stitches. It also
comes in a much wider selection of
sizes and fibres.

Canvas is described according to the
number of threads or holes per 5 cm
(1 in). A rug canvas with a very open
weave and large holes will obviously
give a coarser, bolder effect than a
very fine canvas with twenty-eight
holes per 5 cm (1 in).

Canvas can be bought by the metre
and comes in varying widths and
fibres. Natural fibres like linen are
more expensive but are softer, more
supple to work and not so harsh on
the thread as synthetic canvas.

THREADS

Any thread can be used for canvas
work as long as it is suitable for its
eventual purpose: for instance a
church kneeler should be made from
a hardwearing yarn like Wilton
carpet thrums or crewel wool.
The thread should completely cover
the canvas. If no specific thread or

canvas is given, or if you are going
to design your own work, then you
should experiment until you find
exactly the right combination: not
so thin that the canvas shows, not so
swollen that the canvas is distorted.
Sometimes several fine yarns can be
used together to achieve the desired
effect. Don't try to save time by using
too long a thread in your needle: the
canvas may wear it thin and give
you an uneven result. It is best to
keep the thread length *very* short in
synthetic canvas.

NEEDLES

Use blunt ended, long-eyed tapestry
needles of the appropriate size.

STARTING OFF

Make a slip knot at the end of the
yarn, leave it on the WS a few holes
away from where you are starting.
When you come back with the end
of your first stitch, split the yarn
with your needle. This helps anchor
the thread. Cut the original knot off
later when the thread is well covered
by later stitches.

STITCHES

There are literally dozens of canvas
work stitches. For our projects we
have picked out some of the most
important ones, concentrating on
those giving immediate effects. Some
stitches produce interesting textures,
some make interesting patterns,
some are high-relief stitches, some lie
flat on the canvas.

IN GENERAL

A simple rectangular wooden frame
will keep work free from distortion.
Attach the canvas by stapling.
If your design depends on counting,
stick to counting either threads, *or*
holes to minimise confusion.
If you are covering large areas, for
instance in tent stitch, it is easy to
miss a hole. Holding the work to the
light will reveal any gaps.
Mask the edges of the canvas with
tape to prevent it unravelling while
you are working.
Whatever the shape of the final
design, work it on a rectangular
canvas so that you can put it on a
frame. Cut the shape itself later.
Always leave really ample turnings
for stretching and mounting.

Canvas work chair seat

There are often times when a good chair or stool needs a new fabric seat. Here, a simple unit of embroidery is repeated to fit the shape desired. Any remaining irregular shapes and those that turn an edge have simply been treated with tent stitch. The design depends on texture and tonal value for interest rather than on colour emphasis.

MATERIALS

Canvas Single thread linen, twelve holes to 2.5 cm (1 in)

Thread A mixture of unbleached Patons Capstan knitting yarn, DMC white perlé number 5 and Appleton's crewel yarn shade 992. Quantities will vary according to size of chair. Ours is approximately 38 cm (15 in) square. It took one ball (50 g) Patons Capstan, five 10 g balls perlé number 5 and twenty-eight skeins crewel wool

Tapestry needle number 16

METHOD

1 Remove the existing cover and use it to make a pattern for the new seat. Measure the amount of canvas you will need, allowing generous turnings, but keep the canvas in a rectangular shape for working.

2 Mask the canvas edges with tape and staple it to the frame. Find the middle by counting threads. Mark it with a felt-tip pen.

3 Work the first square, starting in the middle:
Work berlin star stitch over six threads of canvas in one thickness of Capstan yarn.
Work cross stitch all round this square over a single thread of canvas in a double thread of perlé.
Now work twelve squares of algerian eye over four threads of canvas with a double thread of crewel wool. Surround this by twenty squares of berlin star stitch in double thread crewel wool. Unlike the central star this should be worked over only four threads of the canvas.
Now work two rows of tent stitch all round the outside of the square using four threads of crewel wool.

4 Divide the blocks of different

stitches with back stitch in perlé over one thread of canvas.

5 Work a single french knot in the centre of each algerian eye with perlé in two thicknesses. The knot needs only one twist of the needle.

6 Repeat the unit until the canvas is covered.

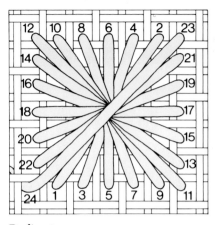

Berlin star

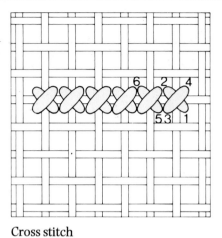

Cross stitch

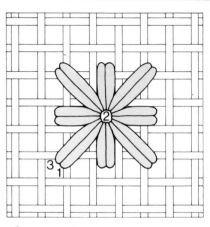

Algerian eye

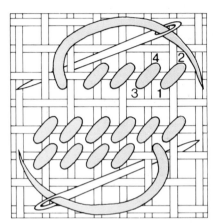

Tent stitch

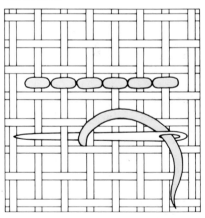

Back stitch

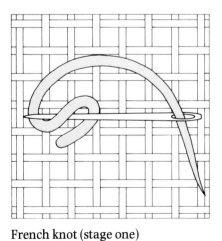

French knot (stage one)

(stage two)

Making up
Stretch if necessary (see page 8).
Canvas work can be used for any
type of chair seat. Apply it to the
chair exactly as you would any other
heavy upholstery fabric, according
to the design of your chair.

Rug
in canvas work

This rug uses the same unit of stitches as the chair seat but an entirely different effect is gained by altering the scale and using a mixture of Laine-à-broder and Wilton thrums for the threads

MATERIALS

Canvas Double-thread rug canvas four holes to 2.5 cm (1 in) not less than 84 cm × 53 cm (33 in × 21 in)

Thread Laine-à-broder in 25 g hanks
DMC 7146 Tan, four hanks, plus six extra for fringe
DMC 7207 Mulberry, nine hanks, plus six extra for fringe
DMC 7164 Pale Tan, four hanks
DMC 7104 Shrimp Pink, twenty-five hanks
Wilton carpet thrums: a small amount of wine and deep turquoise

Tapestry needle number 14

METHOD

Mark the centre of the canvas by counting threads and work fifteen units. The stitches are the same as for the chair seat, using this yarn:
Central berlin star in double thickness tan.
Cross stitch in surrounding row double thickness pale tan.
Algerian eye in double thread of Wilton thrums in wine.
Small berlin star in double thickness mulberry.
Tent stitch in four thickness pink.
French knots in single thread of Wilton thrums in turquoise.

Back stitch in a single thread of shrimp pink.

Finishing

1 Stretch if necessary (see page 8).
2 Trim the edges to 4 cm (1½ in) and then turn the raw edges under, allowing an unembroidered double thread of canvas and one empty hole to show all round.
3 Now make a row of velvet stitch (see below) with a double thickness, one of wine and one of tan Laine-à-broder over a 13 cm (5 in) strip of card to form a fringe.

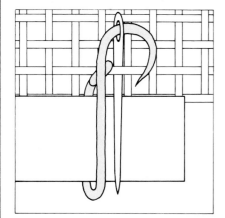

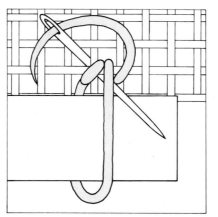

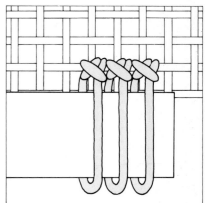

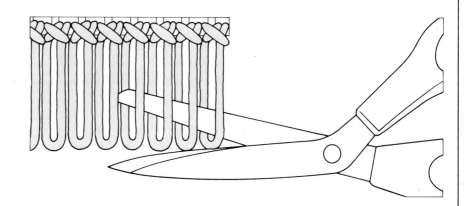

Canvas work cushion

This 38 cm (15 in) cushion with thirty-six units of embroidery has been worked in exactly the same way as the white chair seat. This time the effect is quite different because bright colours have been used.

MATERIALS

Canvas Single-thread linen, 12 holes to 2.5 cm (1 in). A piece measuring 43 cm (17 in) square to allow for turnings.

Thread Three hanks Laine tapisserie 7742
Eight 25 g balls any mixed 3-ply knitting or weaving yarn in orange
Seventeen hanks DMC Laine tapisserie 7243 in purple
Thirteen skeins DMC perlé 606 (number 3) in scarlet
One skein DMC perlé 3688 (number 5) in pink

An extra two hanks scarlet perlé to make a twisted cord (optional)

Tapestry needle number 16

Material for backing fabric (we used purple velvet)

METHOD

1 The stitches and their position are the same as for the chair seat shown on page 26.
Use the coloured threads this way:
Central berlin star in orange Laine tapisserie, used single.
Algerian eye in orange 3-ply knitting wool, used single.
Small berlin star squares in purple Laine tapisserie, used single.
Cross stitch, back stitch, tent stitch in scarlet perlé, used single.
French knots in pink perlé, used single.
2 Work thirty-six units.
3 Stretch and finish (see pages 8 and 9).
4 Make a twisted cord (see page 9) from four strands of scarlet perlé and attach with tiny catch stitches.

Little box
in canvas work

*Little boxes are always popular both to work and to give as presents.
In this one, the three-dimensional object itself mixes well with the
textured effects of the stitches.*

For all its apparent complexity, only two stitches are used for the box – velvet and tent stitch. The neat, low-lying tent stitch throws the plushy velvet stitch into relief. The thread is cotton perlé throughout. The soft colour is achieved by sometimes using two different colours in the needle at once.

The embroidered part of the box is worked in three pieces: the circular top of the lid, a strip to make the outside edge of the lid, and a strip the same size which curves round to make the side of the box itself. The lid rests on a protruding inner 'lip' made from card and fabric which sits inside the box.

MATERIALS

Canvas Single thread linen twelve holes to 2.5 cm (1 in), large enough to cover line drawing plus generous turnings

Thread One skein DMC cotton perlé (weight 5) in the following colours.
Pinks: 223, 3328, 316, 776, 103
Purple: 327
Beige: 644
Greens: 830, 70, 730, 469, 55, 506, 904, 730
Browns: 938, 433

Tapestry needle number 16

Small amount of contrasting fabric such as light curtain weight for base and lining. We used a purple satiny fabric

Light-weight card that will be firm enough for base and sides and yet will also stand up to being bent without cracking

METHOD

The embroidery

1 Cut a suitable area of canvas. You may have a piece big enough to put all three areas on at once, or you may need to work each separately. Mask the edges with tape to prevent it unravelling.
2 Lay the canvas over the circle on page 33 and carefully trace with a felt-tip pen. The strip on this page should be first traced on to tracing paper. It has been cut to fit our page, so draw first one half and then the other, matching them exactly at the centre to make one long strip. Now cut your tracing in half lengthwise (along the dotted line). Lay the canvas over the strip for the edge of the lid and trace, then do

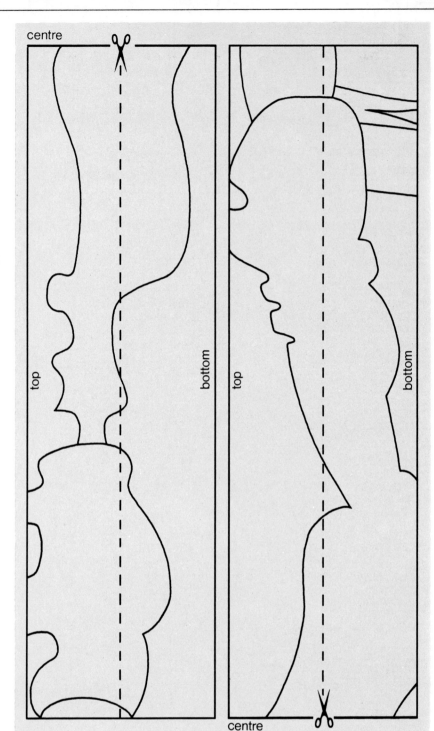

the same for the strip for the box side. Leave some distance between the two to allow for turnings.
3 Attach the canvas to a suitable rectangular frame with staples.
4 Work all the tent stitch areas first. See page 27 for a diagram of the stitch.
5 Always work velvet stitch from the bottom of the shape upwards so that the loops do not have to be lifted out of the way. Detailed instructions for velvet stitch are on page 29, but in this case it is worked over a

knitting needle before cutting, rather than a strip of card.

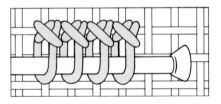

6 When the embroidery is complete, remove the canvas from the frame and cut around the work allowing 2.5 cm (1 in) turnings.

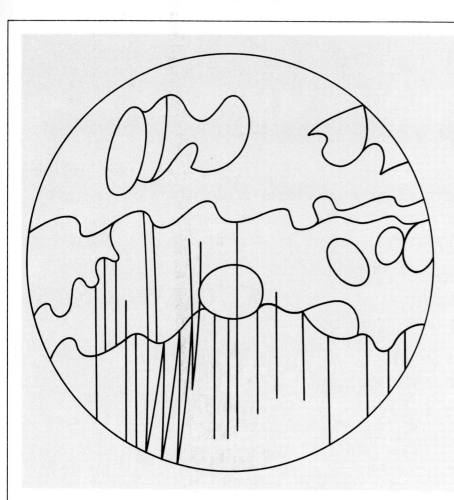

The circle on the left forms the top of the box. The strip on the far left will form *both* the side of the box and the edge of the lid. The strip has been cut in half to fit our page so when you trace it, be careful to match the centre exactly, joining the lines of the design correctly.
When you have traced off one continuous strip, you will then use the top half (above the dotted line) to form the edge of the lid. The bottom half (below the dotted line) forms the side of the box.

Making up the box

Top

1 Cut a card circle 11 cm (4⅜ in) diameter. Pin the work to the card so that the two circles exactly coincide.
2 Lace the edges of the canvas over the card from side to side with spare perlé thread.

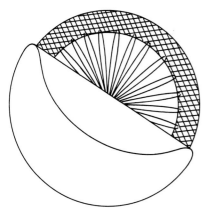

3 Now cut a circle of lining fabric allowing 1 cm (½ in) turnings. Turn the edges under and pin. Invisibly catch stitch to the underside of the lid around its circumference. Remove the tacking.

Outside edge of top

1 Cut a piece of card measuring 35.5 × 2.5 cm (14 in × 1 in).
2 Lay the strip of card on WS of embroidered strip, fold over the edges and lace while flat.
3 Fold and catch stitch the narrow ends.
4 Cut a piece of lining fabric the same size as the card plus turnings. Turn under the edges, pin and slip stitch to the embroidered strip.
5 Bend the strip round to match the circular top of the box and attach the two with small overcasting stitches. Join the little upright seam.

Base

1 Cut a second identical card circle and two pieces of lining fabric slightly larger. Lace a layer of fabric over the card, as before. Turn under the raw edges of the second piece of lining fabric, pin and slip stitch to the rest of the base.
2 Now take the second embroidered strip, treat exactly as the first one, attaching to the base as described for the top of the box.

Inner 'lip'

Cut a strip of card 32.5 cm × 4.5 cm (12¾ in × 1¾ in) and cover with lining fabric as with base. Bend and catch stitch the short edges together and set inside the lower half of box to form a lip on which the lid can rest. It should not need stitching or glueing to stay in place.

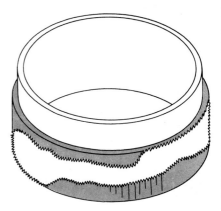

Mirror frame in velvet stitch

Velvet stitch in perlé cotton is used once again for a different effect. This was inspired by bulb fields in Spring. The drawing only shows the main areas of colour – you may want to choose your own.

MATERIALS

Canvas Single linen thread, twelve holes to 5 cm (1 in), enough to cover the design plus generous turnings

Thread DMC perlé cotton number 5 We used one skein each of the following:
Yellows: 611, 137
Greens: 913, 509, 469, 732, 319, 904, 501, 924, 991, 320
Scarlet: 608
Pinks: 316, 776
Mauve: 208
Grey: 3023

Mounting board

Fine string for lacing

Lining fabric for back of frame

Piece of mirror 1 cm ($\frac{1}{2}$ in) bigger all round than the rectangular space in the middle of the frame

Two curtain rings

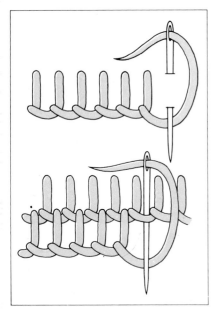

METHOD

1 Work the embroidery in velvet stitch throughout, mixing colours as you like. The stitch is worked over a knitting needle as for the little box (see page 32).

2 Remove the work from the frame and cut round the embroidered sections leaving a generous 2.5 cm (1 in) all round.
Stretch if necessary (see page 8).

3 Draw the exact outline of the embroidered section of the mirror frame onto heavy weight mounting board. Cut it out using a steel rule and a Stanley knife.

4 Snip the four inner corners of the canvas almost to the embroidery.

5 Fold over the board and lace all round with fine string.

6 Cut a lining 1 cm ($\frac{1}{2}$ in) bigger all round than the embroidered section and snip into the inner corners. Fold under the raw edges, put a few pins in to hold them in place, then slip stitch the lining to the embroidery.

7 Put the mirror in position and secure it in place by working four rows of detached blanket stitch (see previous page) around the four sides. The first row of stitches enter the material, the second and subsequent rows do not.

8 Sew two curtain rings firmly to the back if you want to hang up the mirror.

Choker
in canvas work

This small piece shows one more variation of velvet stitch and tent stitch combined. This time it is used on a fine French canvas twenty-eight holes to 2.5 cm (1 in). It has been worked in three threads of stranded cotton in dark grey, mauve and turquoise.

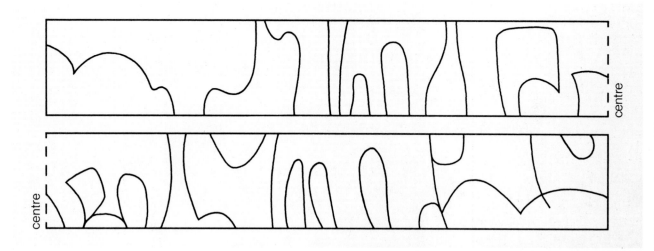

You could copy the general effect of our choker from the photograph or line drawing. Alternatively, you could design your own. One way of doing this would be to take a piece of card and cut a 'window' strip out of it exactly the size of the finished choker. Move this 'window' around on magazine photographs until you get a combination of lines, colours and textures you like. Trace off the main areas of colour on to your canvas with a felt-tip pen.

MATERIALS

Canvas 30 cm × 2.5 cm (12 in × 1 in) plus turnings

Thread We used DMC stranded cotton (three strands). One hank of each of the following:
Turquoise: 995   Grey: 844
Purple/Mauve: 550, 208

Heavy sew-in interfacing of the same dimension but minus the amount for turnings

1 m of 2.5 cm (1 in) velvet ribbon

METHOD

1 If you use our design, place the canvas over the drawing above and trace. The design is shown in two halves in order to fit the page size, so be careful to join exactly at the centre.
2 Use velvet and tent stitch as in the canvas box (page 32). Work the embroidery on a frame. Rather than waste canvas, the small area required can be sown on to a piece of odd material to bring it to a practical size for your frame. Staple it to the frame in the usual way.
3 Stretch if necessary (see page 8).
4 Trim the canvas and lace it on to heavy-weight interfacing.
5 Find the centre of the velvet ribbon and pin to the centre of the canvas. Slip stitch neatly all round, leaving the ends of the ribbon to flow beyond the embroidered section.

Belt
in canvas work

*A simple repeating pattern in tones of one colour, inspired by the
small flower head of the aubrietia.*

MATERIALS

Canvas A strip of eighteen holes to
2.5 cm (1 in), 10 cm (4 in) wide plus
turnings of 2.5 cm (1 in) times the
exact waist measurement. *NB*
measure the waist *over* whatever
clothes will be worn with the belt

Heavy sew-in interfacing: a strip as
above but minus the turnings.

Lining Gros-grain or ordinary ribbon
the exact dimensions of the finished
embroidery

Thread One ball each of the
following:
3-Suisses Mimizan crochet thread in
lilac, used single
Twilleys Stalite No 3 cotton in
purple, used single
Dewhurst silk perlé 809 pinky lilac,
used single
Robin Moonlight Glitter in purple,
used double

Tapestry needle number 18

Trouser fastener

METHOD

1 Prepare the canvas by stapling to
a frame.
2 Work the repeat design using the
stitches and colours given in the
diagrams on the next page.
3 Stretch (see page 8).
4 Turn the raw edges of the canvas
over the interfacing and catch stitch.
Put the ribbon over WS canvas and
slip stitch neatly all round.
5 Sew on a trouser fastener so that
the two short edges of the belt
meet and just overlap.

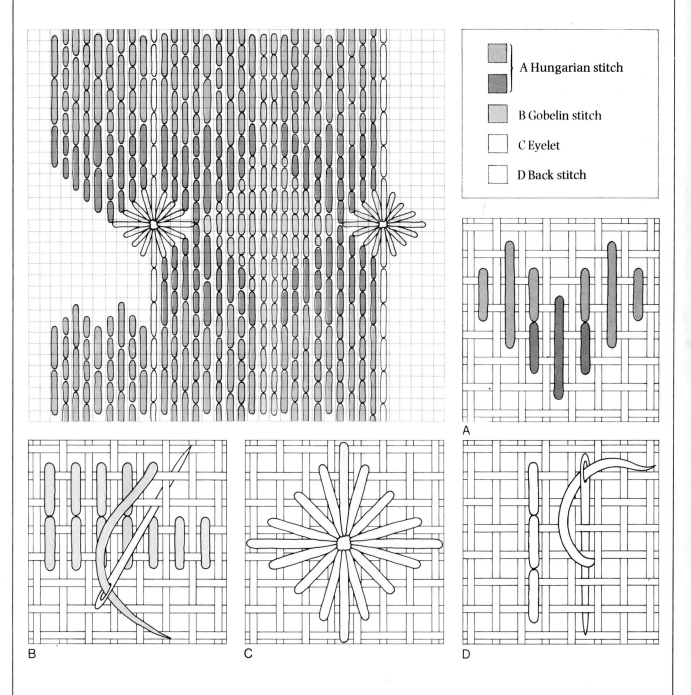

A Hungarian stitch

B Gobelin stitch

C Eyelet

D Back stitch

A

B

C

D

Patchwork

Patchwork is a popular technique traditionally associated
with regular geometric shapes. One technique we show here
is a departure from tradition as it uses an assymetrical
and 'representational' image, traced on to sew-in interfacing.
Each piece is then carefully cut away and used as a
template. The raw edges are turned over and invisibly
caught to the interfacing. The interfacing remains in the
finished work. Each piece is then overcast to the next.
The completed units are then assembled and overcast in
the same way. The technique has many possibilities
and can easily be extended to free-flowing 'organic' shapes.
The fabrics should be of the same or similar weight and
type which will minimize washing and wearing difficulties
and will be far easier to assemble.

Patchwork bed cover

The inspiration for this design came from looking at houses and roof tops. Seventy repeated units 13 cm × 15 cm (5 in × 6 in) are separated by 5 cm (2 in) bands running both horizontally and vertically. Total size of cover: 1.5 m × 2.2 m (4 ft 10 in × 7 ft 2 in).

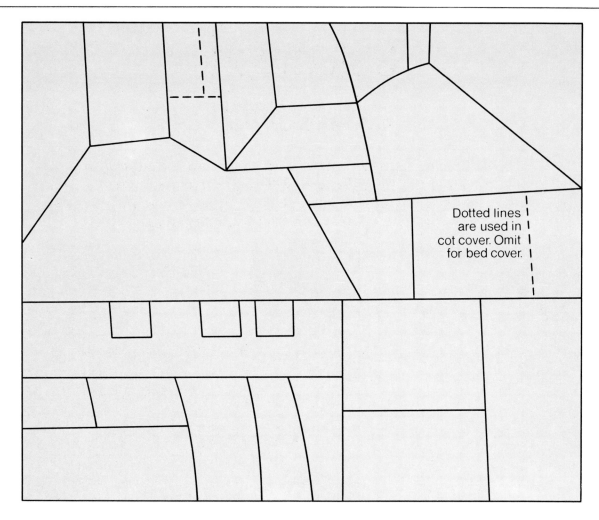

Dotted lines
are used in
cot cover. Omit
for bed cover.

MATERIALS

Viyella throughout in eight different colours. Quantities vary according to shape of template: eg the window shapes are tiny, and take as little as 20 cm (8 in) of a 90 cm cloth. One metre (39 in) is sufficient for the majority of colours but the border and bands that separate the units need 3.70 m (4 yd).

Lining fabric 3 m of 115 cm (3 ft 9 in) 3 m of 115 cm (3 ft 9 in) fabric

Heavy sew-in interfacing 85 cm (33 in) wide × 9.70 m

Sewing cotton in the most dominant colour for making up

Ball-point pen

METHOD

1 Place the interfacing over the line drawing above. Some of the shapes are very small. These could be left out if you prefer.
2 Trace the complete unit with a ball-point pen.
3 Mark each piece of the unit with a vertical arrow parallel to the straight

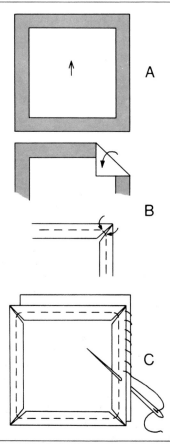

A

B

C

edge of the work. This will help keep the grain straight throughout.
4 Cut out one interfacing shape at a time with small scissors.
5 Place the interfacing shape on the WS of the fabric to be cut and pin it with its directional arrow on the straight grain of the fabric (A).
6 Cut out the fabric allowing an extra 5 mm ($\frac{1}{4}$ in) for turnings (a little less on really tiny shapes and a little more on much bigger ones).
7 With a fine sewing needle, catch these edges over on to the interfacing being very careful to mitre all the corners and catch none of the right side of the fabric (B).
8 As each shape is made, sew it to the neighbouring shape by means of a small overcast stitch with right sides of each piece together (C). Assemble all the pieces of one unit and press gently.
When all units are complete, join them together with 5 cm (2 in) bands of patchwork, finishing with similar strips to form the outside edge of the bed cover.
9 Line back of work as for making up a hanging (see page 9).

Patchwork
cot cover

The same design can be adapted for a cot cover. Here a total of only eighteen units are placed together with no dividing bands to make a cover 51 cm × 81 cm (20 in × 32 in) including the edge. The fabric is again Viyella but this time only five colours have been used.

MATERIALS

50 cm (20 in) each of the most used Viyella colours

20 cm (8 in) of the less used ones (eg see the two darker colours in our design above)

1 m for the edging colour

2.80 m (3 yd) of No 2 piping cord

1 m lining material

50 cm (20 in) of heavy sew-in interfacing

Sewing cotton

Ball-point pen

METHOD

Make up each unit as described in the instructions for the bed cover, but this time join them to each other so that the design is repeated with no dividing band between. Then edge in the following way:

1 Make a strip of Viyella 10 cm wide × 7.40 m (4 in × 8 yd) plus turnings. (You will need to join several strips, using the crossway method described on page 9).

2 Fold the strip in half lengthwise and press the fold. Open out again and seam the short ends together.

3 Refold.

4 Mark the length into 2.5 cm (1 in) divisions, by means of a pencil dot, 1.5 cm ($\frac{5}{8}$ in) from raw edge.

5 Pinch up any one dot and move it towards the next dot on the left. Pin. Do the same with the dot to the right this time moving it to the right. A small box pleat has now been formed which can be repeated all around the strip. Tack these carefully over the whole length.

6 Make a 2.80 m (3 yd) strip of covered piping with a 4 cm (1½ in) width of Viyella. See page 9 for the instructions on making piping.

7 Place the sewing line of the piping to the sewing line of RS cot cover edge. Pin, tack and stitch with zip foot attachment on the machine.

8 Now place the pleated edging RS to RS of the cot cover, raw edge level with the piping raw edge. Pin all the way round, tack and sew, again with the zip foot in order to get close to the cord. Turn all the raw edges to the WS and press.

9 Cut out a lining, with a seam allowance all round. Fold raw edges under and attach to the back of the cot cover exactly as described for a hanging (see page 9).

Patchwork tote bag

The same patchwork technique is used here as for the cot cover and bedspread, but the design is different. A patchwork panel is framed in heavy furnishing cotton. The handles are strong enough for the bag to carry heavy books or shopping.

MATERIALS

Collection of printed and plain scraps of cotton fabric for the two panels of patchwork on the front and back of the bag. Each completed panel should measure 36 cm × 37 cm (14 in × $14\frac{1}{2}$ in) plus turnings

1 m furnishing fabric for plain areas, handles and lining. Cut the following strips, allowing 1.5 cm ($\frac{5}{8}$ in) seam allowances on all pieces:
Two 7.5 cm × 38 cm (3 in × 15 in), for the handles
Two 36 cm × 18 cm (14 in × 7 in), for the top
Two 36 cm × 4 cm (14 in × $1\frac{1}{2}$ in), for the bottom
Four 58.5 cm × 5 cm (23 in × 2 in), for the sides

Two 38 cm (15 in) lengths of 5 cm (2 in) webbing

Four lengths of 38 cm (15 in) number 3 piping cord

Heavy sew-in interfacing, enough to cover the design twice

Cartridge paper

Tracing paper

Tacking cotton

Sewing cotton to match the plain fabric colour for making up

METHOD

1 Trace and enlarge the design on page 45, or trace and draw your own on to cartridge paper. The method for enlarging is described on page 7.
2 Trace the design twice on to the interfacing (you will need two copies for the front and back of the bag).
3 Assemble the design using the same technique described for the bed cover (see page 42).
4 Press.

44

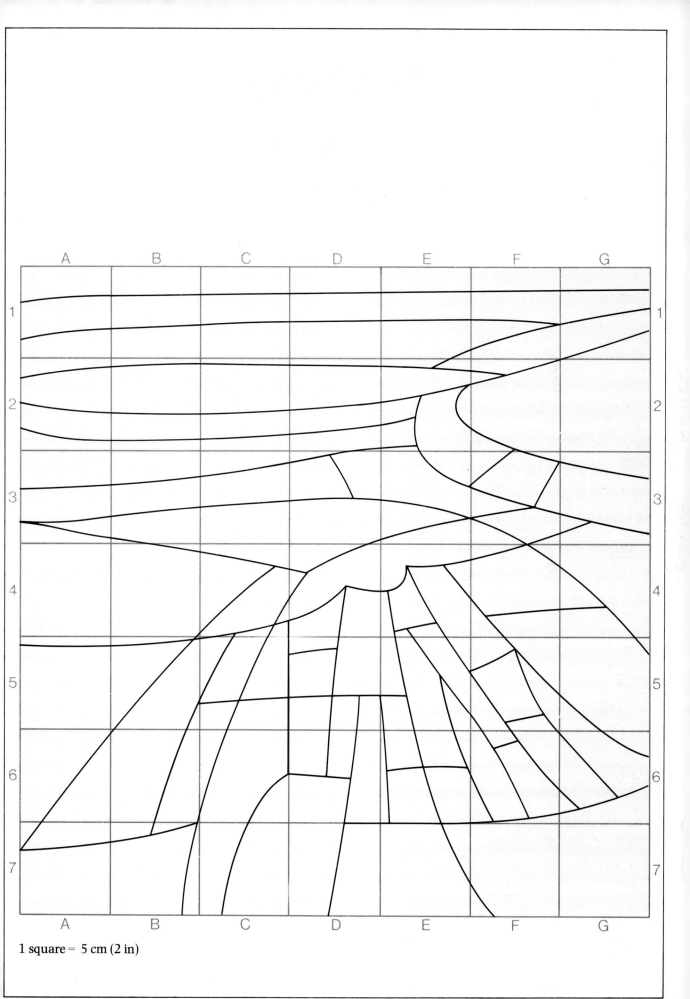

1 square = 5 cm (2 in)

Assembling the bag

Front and back the same

1 Take the completed patchwork piece which should measure 36 cm × 37 cm (14 in × 14½ in) and 'frame' it in the strips of furnishing fabric, as shown right, using small machine stitches.

2 Press all seams open.

3 Place the front and back RS together and join the bottom seam. Press it open.

4 Open the work out flat. Remove the small rectangular pieces of fabric (see diagram).

5 Fold again RS together.

6 Sew both the side seams. To form the width in the bottom of the bag, place RS together, matching the side seams to the fold lines. Stitch this open end with a 1 cm (½ in) seam.

Handles (both the same)

1 Prepare four lengths of piping cord 38 cm (15 in) long.

2 Take one of the remaining strips 7.5 cm × 38 cm (3 in × 15 in) fabric. Chalk a centre line along the length.

3 Fold one edge at a time over the piping cord and up to the chalk line.

4 Stitch with zip foot attachment close to the cord.

5 Lay a length of webbing inside and between the two stitched lines allowing the two raw-edged turnings to come together. Zigzag over this join between the two raised edges on the WS.

6 Pin the handles in position on RS bag, raw edges resting on top line of the bag and 13 cm (5 in) in from the side fold of the bag. Then stitch.

Lining

1 Cut a lining 1.15 m × 45 cm (45 in × 18 in) plus 1.5 cm (⅝ in) seam allowance all round and follow the same instructions for the side seam and gusset.

2 Press, and turn to RS.

3 Fold in and tack the top raw edges on the bag and lining.

4 Place lining in bag. Tack together around the top. Machine all round on the fold. This will give an added strength to the construction.

5 Remove tackings. Press.

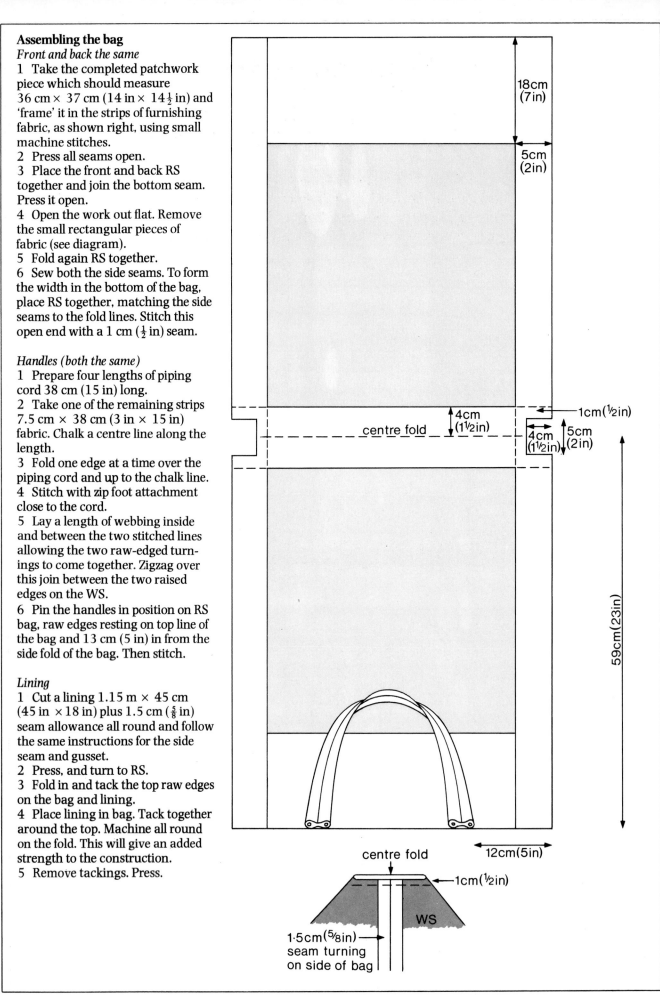

18cm (7in)

5cm (2in)

4cm (1½in)

centre fold

1cm (½in)

4cm (1½in)

5cm (2in)

59cm (23in)

centre fold

1cm (½in)

WS

12cm (5in)

1·5cm (⅝in) seam turning on side of bag

Patchwork
cushion in shot silks

This effective cushion is made up of four repeated 20 cm (8 in) units using shot fabric with the grain going in different directions. The technique is 'English' patchwork, where paper shapes, later discarded, are used to back the fabric during sewing.

MATERIALS

Small amounts Thai silk or other fabric with a 'shot' surface

Cartridge paper

Ruler

Pencil

Sewing cottons

Tracing paper

Tailor's chalk

Fine pins

METHOD

1 Draw a 20 cm (8 in) square on the cartridge paper. Using a ruler, rule some stripes of random widths down the square. Now divide each stripe into smaller rectangles. When you are happy with the design, copy it three times on to more cartridge paper. A simple way to do this: use tracing paper and a thick pencil to copy the design. Put the tracing *pencil-side* down on the cartridge paper, and go over the lines from the back with a harder pencil or ball-point pen. This will transfer the first pencil lines to the cartridge paper. Our design (to be enlarged) is shown right, if you want to use it.

2 Cut out the first small rectangle from the cartridge paper to form a template for cutting the fabric. Pin the template on the fabric. Cut out the fabric slightly larger than the paper shape all round (the amount will vary with the fabric – 5 mm ($\frac{1}{4}$ in) would be enough for a fabric which does not fray readily).

3 Turn all the raw edges over the cartridge paper template and tack. Keep the corners neat (A).

4 Cut out the next rectangle in the same stripe, using the same colour. Treat it in the same way.

5 Place the two units RS together and join one seam in tiny over-casting stitches (B).

6 Carry on in this way completing the first stripe, but make occasional variations in the grain (C). *Note* The 'straight' grain of a fabric is the vertical direction of strong 'warp' threads parallel to the selvedge of the material. You can see 'grain' lines as visible vertical lines on most fabrics.

7 Start on the next stripe in the design, and so on. Join each stripe together, also using overcasting stitches, until the 20.5 cm (8 in) unit is complete.

8 Make the three units.

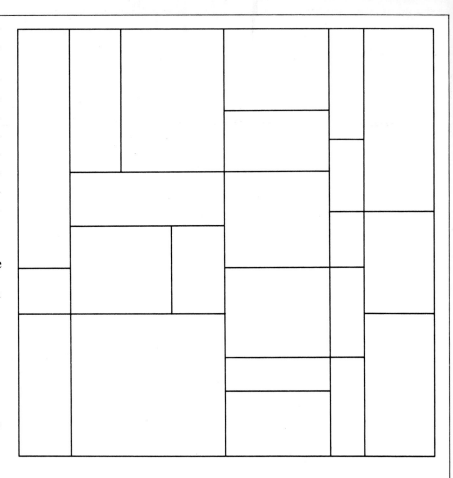

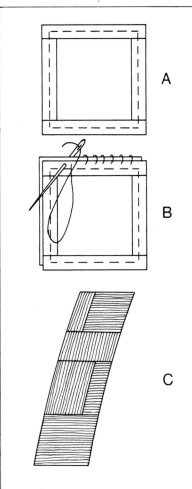

A

B

C

Assembling the units

1 You can arrange the four units any way you like. Try them out in different ways until you find one that pleases you.

2 Join them together using small overcasting stitches.

3 Press lightly, then remove all the template papers.

4 Make up into cushion (see page 9 for instructions).

Stitchery

*If you have some experience of working with traditional
ironed-on transfers and stranded cottons on linen, you
will probably already have considerable knowledge of many
embroidery stitches. If not, the basic stitches are not
difficult to learn and can be perfected with a little practice.
There are many excellent reference books (we give a few on page 9)
which describe more stitches than we can give here.
In fact it is probably much better to learn one stitch really well
and then to experiment with all its possibilities
than to half-learn dozens.*

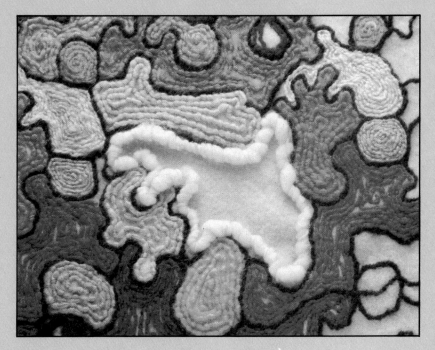

Decorated blanket

Here an old, but well preserved, wool blanket has been couched all over with Wilton carpet thrums in a deep wine red. Then a central band has been treated in a variety of wools that include Wilton thrums, DMC Laine-à-broder and various knitting remnants, some of which have first been made into twisted cords or knotted.

MATERIALS

Blanket
Wools
Chenille needle
Best quality tracing paper
Pencil
French chalk or talcum powder
Crayon in a colour that will show on the blanket
Small pad of felt or similar material

METHOD

1 Trace the whole unit including the outline. Transfer the design using the prick and pounce method (see page 7) with the crayon.

2 Continue moving the tracing paper and repeating the process as many times as the article demands. Remember to move the unit down by 5 cm (2 in) When you repeat it. Match up the lines of the pattern very carefully.

3 Couch the main lines of the design first. The couching method is shown below.

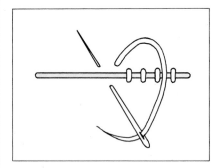

4 Fill the centre panel areas with couched lines in other threads, including hand-made cords (see page 9).

5 Finish the sides with blanket stitch in cream Laine-à-broder.

A close-up of the stitchery on the blanket can be seen on page 49 and on the cover.

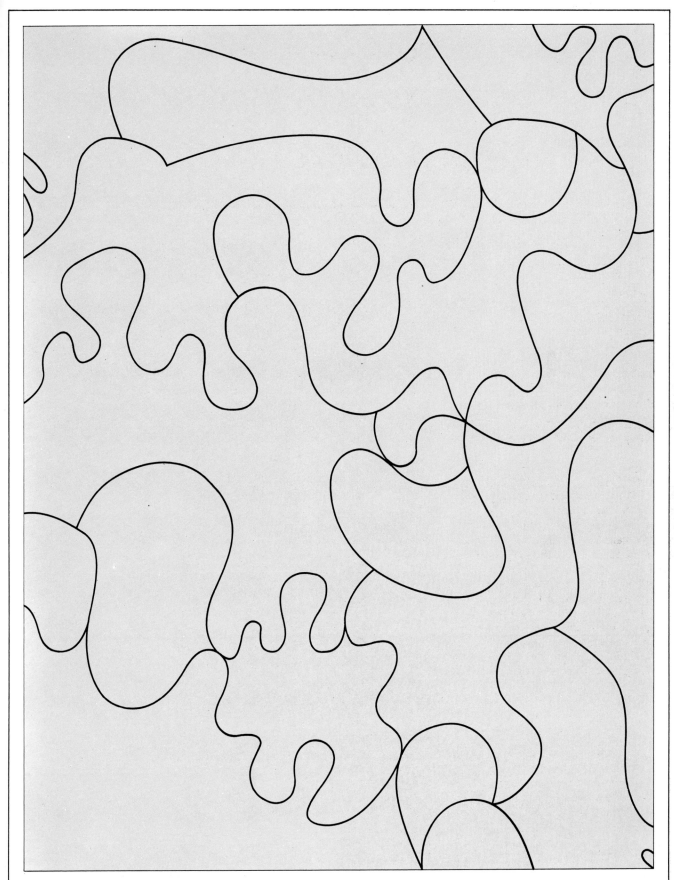

The pattern above is a carefully
worked-out repeat: trace it on best
quality tracing paper and use it as
the basis for design repeat.
Note The pattern has a 5 cm (2 in)
pattern drop.

Embroidered shirts

Stitchery on dress is one of the oldest forms of embroidery, and it still makes a satisfying project: even a tiny area of hand embroidery can individualize something mass produced.

We have used a commercial shirt pattern here and most pattern companies usually have a simple classic like this in their catalogues. We used Simplicity 8785.

The stitch is one of the simplest possible – it is just blanket stitch worked in clusters on various parts of the shirt.

Never cut out any garment until the embroidery is complete and has been stretched.

Match the 'weight' of the thread to the background fabric weight (eg do not weigh down a light weight silk with a heavy wool).

Work on a hoop.

If you have the time and patience, it often helps to make up the garment quickly using an old sheet. This will help you decide which areas to embroider.

MATERIALS

Shirt pattern

Fabric as given on pattern (ours used 2.40 m (7 ft 10½ ins) of 115 cm (3 ft 9 in) fabric)

Embroidery threads according to choice, and weight of fabric

Embroidery hoop

Crewel needle

Rest of requirements according to pattern selected

METHOD

1 The pattern pieces which will be embroidered should be laid on the fabric and a tacked line worked all around these shapes.

2 Remove the pattern pieces and work the embroidery within the tacking lines.

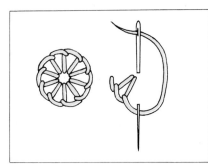

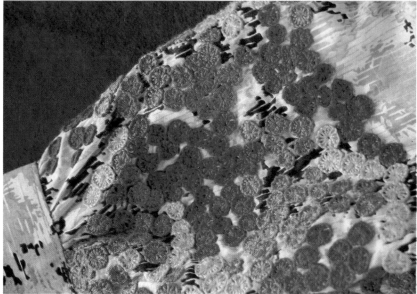

3 When the embroidery is complete, the work should be stretched (see page 8). When dry (after twenty-four hours or so, according to the warmth of the room), remove it from the board. Cut it out and make it up, with the remaining pattern pieces.

The pink moiré shirt
This has an embroidered yoke with stitchery continued in the shot bands down the sleeve. The stitch has been worked in three threads of stranded cotton: DMC Ecru and 819 have been randomly mixed.

The patterned shirt
This has been embroidered on the lower part of the sleeve. The printed pattern on the cloth suggested the random treatment and the colour mixture. Perlé thread number 5 has been used.

Stitchery garden picture

*A small picture of a garden which shows a free and creative use of
wave stitch, cretan stitch, eyelets, couching, straight stitches,
French knots and lazy daisy stitch.*

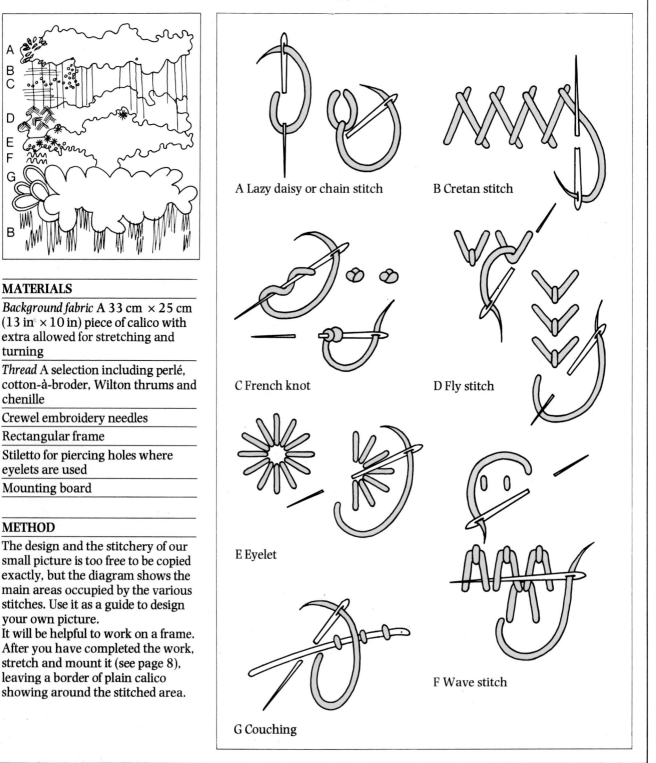

MATERIALS

Background fabric A 33 cm × 25 cm
(13 in × 10 in) piece of calico with
extra allowed for stretching and
turning

Thread A selection including perlé,
cotton-à-broder, Wilton thrums and
chenille

Crewel embroidery needles

Rectangular frame

Stiletto for piercing holes where
eyelets are used

Mounting board

METHOD

The design and the stitchery of our
small picture is too free to be copied
exactly, but the diagram shows the
main areas occupied by the various
stitches. Use it as a guide to design
your own picture.

It will be helpful to work on a frame.
After you have completed the work,
stretch and mount it (see page 8),
leaving a border of plain calico
showing around the stitched area.

A Lazy daisy or chain stitch

B Cretan stitch

C French knot

D Fly stitch

E Eyelet

F Wave stitch

G Couching

54

Braids
and beads

*Most people have scraps of fabrics, threads, knitting wools,
felts, braids, beads and ribbons left over from knitting,
dressmaking and toymaking or bought cheaply as
remnants. These scraps are useful to the embroiderer,
and can form the basis of entire projects.*

Braided cushion and pin cushion

Here is a cushion made from bit-bag scraps. Some of the fabrics have been piped and then trimmed to the sewing line. Some have been frayed or sewn flat to the ground fabric. Others, such as the braids, have been laid flat and sewn with a straight stitch on the machine. Your own experiment will reveal other possibilities.

MATERIALS

Commercial braids, ribbons, velvet and felt strips and other small amounts of contrasting textures of furnishing and dress fabric

Enough fabric to make front and back of cushion

Piping cord

A circular template for round cushion (a round tray would be suitable)

METHOD

To make piping see page 9.
The fabric for covering the piping cord has been cut on the straight grain. Fabrics that do not fray such as felt, leathers and plastics may be cut away (trimmed) down near to the stitching, taking away the turning. *Important* These should still start off large enough to hold satisfactorily, eg a 4 cm ($1\frac{1}{2}$ in) strip is essential for a number 6 piping cord.
Braids and ribbons can be attached flat or folded, gathered or frayed. Lay down your most 'interesting' braid on the fabric first and group the others round it.
Trim off the ends protruding over the edge of the cushion fabric.
Cut out a backing and make up as instructions for cushions (page 9). You can also make a smaller version as a pin cushion. See the photograph on the previous page.

Textured
waistcoat and shawl

This unusual, dramatic but simple technique involves taking as a foundation an ordinary piece of open-weave curtain net, and threading it through with ribbons, wools and surface stitchery.

MATERIALS

Waistcoat pattern –
we used Butterick 6185

1 m cream curtain net (the best is
Scandinavian open weave)

Wools Seven balls of knitting and
crochet yarn in a variety of thick and
fine white, gold, beige and cream
mohairs, crochet cottons and aran
yarn

3 m × 5 mm (10 ft × $\frac{1}{4}$ in) wide
mixed lace and satin ribbon

Tapestry needle with a very large eye

Sewing thread in colour to match
the basic fabric

Satin to make bias strips for binding
and a rouleau belt

Piece of softboard

METHOD

1 Lay the pattern on the net fabric and carefully cut it out. Then pin the pieces to softboard to prevent any 'shrinkage' during working.

2 The method consists of darning in areas with wools and ribbons, then decorating the spaces between.

3 When the 'darned' areas are complete, decorate further with running stitch (shown below), and with french knots and blanket stitch (see pages 53 and 54). Blanket stitch clusters will need to be held down round the edges with a fine couching thread otherwise they tend to bubble up.

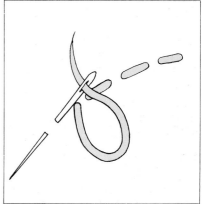

4 As well as purchased ribbons, you can make your own by tearing narrow pieces of suitable fabric and weaving them in too. The aim is to cover the original net completely.

5 Anchor the ends of the ribbons with tiny hand stitches in matching thread.

6 When the embroidery is finished, make up the waistcoat according to the pattern instructions.

7 Finish the raw edges by binding with a narrow bias strip of satin.

Shawl
A simple triangular shape in the same technique using different colours. The size shown here is 1.48 m (4 ft 10 in) on the longest edge. The neck to point depth is 61 cm (24 in).
The top edge is bound as the edges of the waistcoat (above). The two sides have a hand-knotted, fringed edge made from fine machine-knit thread.

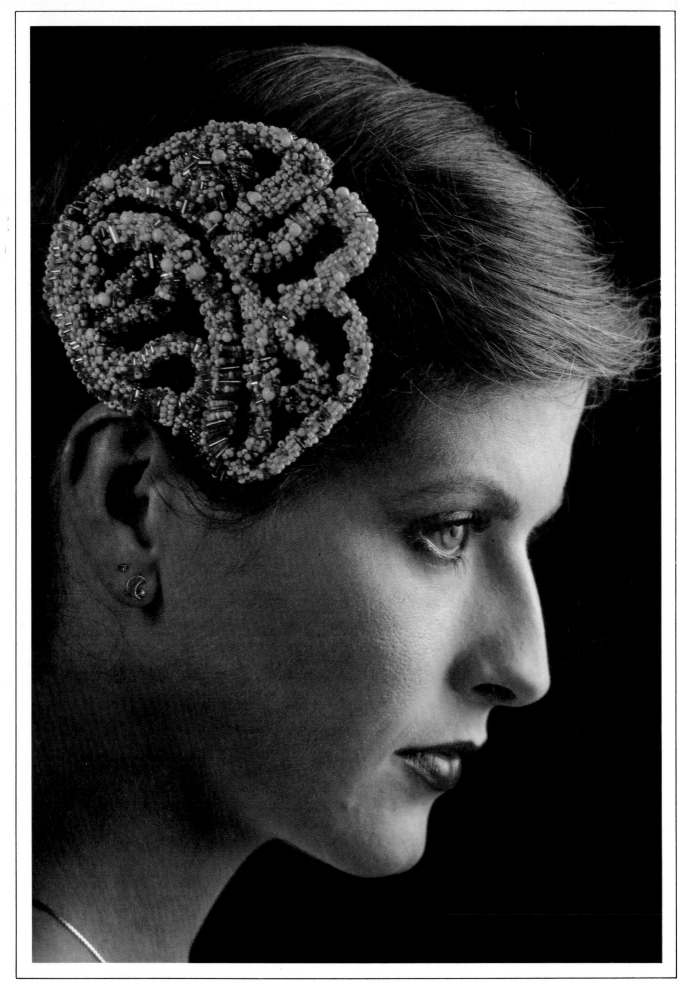

Decorative beaded motif

Beading is a rich decorative technique. The motif shown here could be applied to hair combs, belts, buckles or even used as a movable piece of jewellery. The raised section is worked over a buckrum mould.

MATERIALS

Small area of white or pastel cotton organdie, to fit a 15 cm (6 in) circular embroidery hoop

1 m number 3 piping cord

50 cm (20 in) number 2 piping cord

Beading needle

Any selection of beads

Gutterman pure silk sewing thread, and wax block to pull it over

Buckram circle, 2.5 cm (1 in)

Card

UHU glue

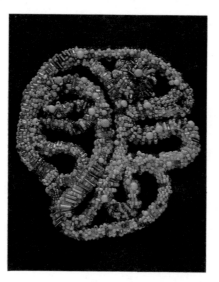

METHOD

Design

1 Lay the piping cord on a piece of stiff card and twist it into a satisfying shape. Taper the ends of the piping cord and glue them together. Also glue any sections touching and supporting each other, otherwise the motif will fall apart when taken off the frame. It must be solid enough when finished to be handled. Use the glue sparingly.

2 Balance the initial shape by adding small lengths of the finer cord in some areas. Leave it to dry.

Preparation

3 Transfer the motif to the mounted organdie. Fasten the motif in place with a tiny amount of glue. Now sew the cord down with absolutely even stitches every 5 mm (¼ in) from both sides of the organdie.

4 Make a small buckrum mould for the raised beaded circle:
Cut a 2.5 cm (1 in) circle of buckrum and soak it in water. Don't get it *too* wet; it should still be pliable. Mould it over the top of a thimble (right). Allow it to dry for 12 hours, and then carefully remove it. Trim the edges evenly.

Beading

5 Thoroughly wax your pure silk thread in order to strengthen it. Now start beading at the top of the work. Pick up enough beads to cover the cord. Keep the beading horizontal. You can mix the beads according to the shade or texture needed. Don't thread a large bead alongside several small ones, otherwise the small ones disappear inside the larger ones and the beading becomes uneven. Six or eight beads will cover one or two thicknesses of cord.

6 When the lines of beading are complete, attach the buckrum mould to the beaded cording by burying the thread in between the beads. Stab-stitch around the circle to fasten it securely to the organdie.

7 Now take your needle up through the centre of the raised shape and thread sufficient small beads to reach the base of the circle. Put your needle in again at the base, pull the thread taut, but not too tightly or the thread will rub and fray the edge of the buckrum. Divide the circle into four quarters for even beading, then fill in each quarter with smaller beads. Avoid coming up in the centre as this will eventually make a hole.

8 Remove the organdie from the frame and carefully cut with fine embroidery scissors all around the motif leaving 5 mm (¼ in) organdie turnings. In the smaller spaces you will only be able to leave turnings of approximately 3 mm (⅛ in).

9 Lay the beaded motif upside down on a piece of felt or a similar thick material. Using a darning needle and small quantities of glue gently and evenly turn the cut organdie edges back onto the reverse side of the work. This method has the effect of reinforcing the beading stitches over the piping cord. The motif can then be made completely detachable and thus used as a brooch, a buckle, or a hair ornament.

Quilting

Quilting is traditionally used for bedcovers and clothing where it provides both warmth and decoration. Today it is still very popular with embroiderers for the sympathetic way it combines with so many other techniques such as appliqué and patchwork. Quilting brings interest and body to fabric. Of all the embroidery techniques, it is one of the simplest but also one of the most dramatic in the way it can transform a surface.

Quilting should always be done on a rectangular frame, either laced or stapled on, to prevent puckering and distortion. The design is applied to the top layer first. The bottom layer is then attached to the frame. Wadding is laid over this, then the top fabric. All three layers are then tacked together all over before the quilting begins. This prevents the three layers sliding about.

Quilting can be finished in various ways. A bound edge made from bias-cut fabric is neat and often suitable for garments like quilted waistcoats. For smaller pieces of quilting eg for cushions, treat the quilted layers as one fabric. Make up in the usual way, but using embroidery scissors trim away the excess bulk of wadding close to the seam.

Designs may be transferred either by tacking from a tracing, or by the prick and pounce method.

MATERIALS

Fabric

Light or medium weight fabrics such as cotton, silk and satin give the best results for quilting.

Wadding

A wide range is now available by the metre. *Polyester wadding* is cheap, washable and comes in 2 oz, 4 oz and 8 oz thicknesses. It is cheap, very springy and slightly more difficult to handle than *cotton wadding* which gives a flatter end result. Cotton wadding is not generally washable. *Wool domette* is a wool and cotton mixture, dry-clean only, ideal where a thin warm layer is needed and pleasant to stitch through. It is difficult to cut accurately as it has such a loose weave, but is ideal for small areas of quilting where several layers can be used at once.

ENGLISH QUILTING

This is done with a three-layer sandwich: top fabric, wadding, bottom fabric. The three layers are tacked together all over, and the quilted design is then outlined in back stitch or running stitch by hand. English Quilting can also be done by machine without a frame, using the ordinary presser foot.

TRAPUNTO QUILTING

Here the two fabrics (the top and the backing) are stitched together with running stitch. The back is slit and the opening stuffed to raise the shape. The back slit is then overcast. The best stuffing to use for trapunto quilting is *acrylic waste* left over from blanket-making, and available by the bag in craft shops and large department stores. Don't use cotton wool; it is far too lumpy.

'Fried egg' pin cushion

Trapunto quilting forms a fried egg pin cushion. The 'yolk' is made of yellow felt mounted on a cream crepe for the white of the egg. A gathered scrim forms the irregular edge.

MATERIALS

Fragments of fabric

Any small amount of stuffing (eg acrylic waste – *not* cotton wool)

Sewing cotton

METHOD

1 Cut a circular 'yolk' from yellow felt and a slightly bigger 'white' from crepe.

2 Cut two off-white circular pieces for the top and bottom of the pin cushion itself.

3 Apply the 'yolk' to the 'white' with small stitches, then apply this to the off-white pin cushion top.

4 Now back stitch round the circumference of the yolk near the edge and do the same around the inner and outer edge of the white.

5 Turn the work over and slit through two layers (not through the yolk). Stuff the applied shapes, then overcast the slit edges.

6 Stitch the pin cushion top and bottom together leaving a small opening for turning and stuffing.

7 Take a narrow strip of scrim and zigzag the raw edges to prevent them fraying. Gather slightly, and attach round the edge of the pin cushion with slip stitches. Eyelets (page 54) have been used to decorate the edge.

Quilted 'fruit tart' cushion

A very simple 41 cm (16 in) cushion made interesting by the use of English quilting on Thai silk. The design was inspired by fruit tarts.

MATERIALS

Thai silk 45 cm (18 in) square including turnings

Fine unbleached calico of the same size to back the polyester wadding of same size or four thin layers of the calico used together

A lining material, which could be the same silk as the front, with which to back the cushion

Gutterman buttonhole twist thread for quilting

Good quality tracing paper or materials for pricking and pouncing (see page 7)

Chenille needle

METHOD

1 Trace and enlarge the drawing on page 65 or invent and arrange your own 'fruit tart' shapes on the square. Transfer the design on to the fabric, using the prick and pounce method.

2 Carefully tack the layers together. (Thai silk on top of the wadding with the calico on the lowest level). Tacking should be from the centre outwards working in rectangular blocks of about 5 cm (2 in).

3 With the pattern lines in place and the tacking complete, quilt along the lines with either running stitch (page 59) or back stitch (page 19). Whichever stitch is selected it is important that the needle always enters the fabric in a single stabbing vertical movement (see diagrams, right). Several movements must not be attempted at one time.

4 When the embroidery is complete, gently stretch (page 8). Make up (page 9).

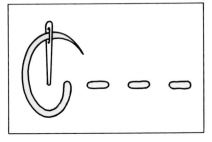

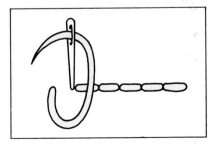

1 square = 2.5 cm (1 in)

Quilted
flower cushion

*This cushion is machine-quilted with random curving lines on silk.
Some of the flowers and leaves can be padded, zigzagged, cut out and
applied separately. The finished size is 40 cm × 40 cm
(16 in × 16 in).*

MATERIALS

Fabric Silk throughout.
Choose a silk that does not fray easily such as shantung.
50 cm (20 in) of 90 cm width for main part cushion
50 cm (20 in) of 90 cm width for flowers and piping
20–30 cm (8–12 in) for leaves
50 cm (20 in) muslin for backing quilted section
50 cm (20 in) of 4-oz polyester wadding

Threads No 50 or No 60 machine embroidery thread in matching or contrasting colours.
Anchor stranded cottons to embellish flowers and leaves

Needles No 11 or 12 ball-point machine needle and a fine crewel needle for hand embroidery

Fine piping cord

Tailor's chalk

Tracing paper

Pencil

METHOD

Preparing the fabric
1 Cut the silk for the main part of the cushion. Allow an extra 4–5 cm 1½–2 in) all round for 'shrinkage' and any possible slight distortion to the shape.
2 Now prepare the fabric with the design. You could make your own by looking at flowers in your garden, or trace our flower and leaf shapes twice, cut them out, and arrange them on the background fabric. The third flower is made from the same shape and attached separately. Pin them in position, and then tack them on to the background.
The curving arrangement we used is shown on the next page. The diagram also shows areas which are hand embroidered later.
3 Draw some random, curving lines in tailor's chalk diagonally across the rest of the cushion.
4 Cut the wadding and muslin the same size as the silk.
Pin all three layers together with the wadding in the middle. Tack them together with large stitches from the centre outwards. Don't overdo the tacking or it will tangle in the foot of the machine later.
Put pins at 7.5 cm (3 in) intervals all round the sides and a few more between the tacked sections. You

can remove these pins as you reach them when machining.

Machining the background pattern
In general, feed the fabric gently through the machine. Don't stretch or pull it, or it will pucker.
Experiment first on a spare piece of cloth using a fairly large straight machine stitch and the normal presser foot.
1 Start machining the random lines from the centre. When you reach the edge, leave the needle in the fabric, lift the lever foot, turn, and put the foot down again and machine your second line. Aim for a soft diagonal

movement across the fabric, relating the curved lines to one another. Continue until you have made random lines all over the background area not covered by the leaves and flowers.
2 Outline the leaves and veins in the same way with straight machine stitch.
3 Now edge the leaves and flowers in small zigzag stitch, changing the colours as appropriate. The zigzag should narrow as it comes to the points of leaves.

1 square = 2.5 cm (1 in)

Making relief appliqué leaves and flowers

1 Trace the flower and leaf shapes. Transfer the leaf shape to a small rectangular piece of silk. Make a sandwich, with the silk underneath and on top of the wadding. Pin in the centre and tack all round the shape. Remove the tracing paper.

2 Machine straight stitch first, then fairly close satin stitch all round the shape. Use the normal presser foot, but sew slowly, manipulating the fabric as you go.

3 Trim close to the shapes with embroidery scissors.

4 Now work a second row of small zigzag stitches – not too close or it may catch in the feed – to neaten any raw edges. Slowly move the leaf shape over the teeth, presser foot down, using your fingers to guide.

5 Embellish with any hand stitchery as desired : eg french knots or long and short straight stitches in one or two strands of stranded cotton.

6 Treat the flowers in the same way.

7 Arrange the flowers and leaves as a unit, stitch them together from the WS with tiny stitches, then attach them to the main part of the cushion in the same way.

Finishing

1 Embellish the flat flowers and leaves with hand stitchery.

2 Stretch the work (see page 8). Measure the edges and square up again if necessary.

3 Make up the cushion with piping

(see page 9). Trim away the wadding to seam the line after attaching the piping and before completing the making up.

Quilted evening bag

This quilted evening bag is made using the same techniques and the same flower and leaf shapes. The raw edges are bound and the strap is made from three plaited rouleau strips. The bag is closed with a rouleau tie fastening.

MATERIALS

Fabric 1 m Jap silk or silk twill for the bag, lining, binding and the rouleau strap and tie fastening

Small pieces of silk for flowers and leaves

30 cm (12 in) muslin

30 cm (12 in) wadding

Threads, needles and design materials as for cushion, page 66. Also some tiny beads

Cartridge paper to make bag pattern

METHOD

1 Enlarge our outline drawing on page 70 on to cartridge paper to make the bag pattern.

2 Cut out a rectangular shape from silk, wadding and muslin measuring 38 cm × 25 cm (15 in × 10 in). Pin the traced bag shape to the silk and tack all round it. *Don't* cut the silk at this stage.

3 Quilt the background and the flower shapes as given for cushion. *Note* the flower and leaves need to be reduced slightly for the smaller bag shape.

4 Now cut out the bag shape. Place the cut out bag on the lining, pin, and draw round it with tailor's chalk and cut it out.
Place the lining and bag sections (both still opened out) WS together. Tack and machine 5 mm ($\frac{1}{4}$ in) in from the edge.

5 Cut bias strips 2 cm ($\frac{3}{4}$ in) wide from the background fabric and join to make a strip long enough to go right round the bag and top (see page 9 for crossway strips method). To bind the straight edge: place RS binding to RS top edge of bag. Tack and machine. Cut any extra binding off. Turn under raw edge of binding and fold to WS of the bag. Hem.

1 square = 2.5 cm (1 in)

6 To make the straps: cut three strips on the straight grain in the same or different colours, each measuring 1.17 m × 4 cm (3 ft 10 in × 1½ in). Fold RS together and machine down the long side and one short end. Pull through to RS using a small safety pin and stout thread.
Make another two identical rouleau strips, then plait the three together. Neaten the raw edges with zigzags and trim off the excess.
7 Fold the bag into shape. Place the straps at the sides of the bag and machine them in place.
8 Tack the side seams with WS bag together,
9 Tack the binding RS to RS bag, raw edges together all the way round. Machine Press, and fold over the raw edge of the bag. Turn under the raw edge of the binding on to the other side of bag. Tack, then hem all round neatening the binding. Join with slip stitches. Press.
10 Make another two rouleau strips 20 cm (8 in) long for the fastening. Attach one to the centre of the flap and the other to the front of the bag. Cover the end attached to the bag front with a cluster of small beads (see photograph, right).

11 Work the additional embroidery on the flower and leaf shapes adding more small beads. Attach to the flap of the bag.

Note The binding of our bag has been finished by zig zagging. This is difficult: only attempt it if you are skilled and experienced.

Machine embroidery

This technique is widely used by modern embroiderers because it offers rich textural and linear effects that are not obtainable any other way. Almost any powered *machine however old, can produce free machine embroidery, though a modern zigzag machine has much more scope.*

PREPARING THE MACHINE

Remove the presser foot and then cover up the fabric 'feed' either by dropping it out of action or by covering it with a darning plate, though this varies with the make of machine: refer to your instruction book if in doubt. The basic difference between this and the normal way of sewing is that *you* must move the fabric. It takes practice to become really competent at free machine embroidery.

The secrets of success are:

Preparing the hoop frame properly
In the case of a wooden ring, bind the edge of the inner ring with bias tape to give a really tight fit. Place the fabric WS up over the inner ring. Place the outer ring over it.

Working on really taut fabric
Gently ease the fabric all round until it is really taut. The inner ring may

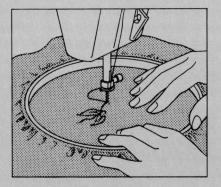

rest a little lower than the outer one, but never the other way round otherwise the work may be lifted off the machine bed and the cotton will be broken. There should be no distortions in the fabric grain. The work really must be as tight as a drum. Tighten it by placing the hoop against your body and gently but firmly pull the work on the opposite side. Rotate the hoop until the fabric is well pulled all round.

Remembering to put the lever down
You will have already removed the presser foot and covered the feed. Put the hoop RS up, flat on the machine. *Now lower the presser foot lever, even though the presser foot is not there.* Without this the machine cannot function properly because its top tension will not be engaged.

Using the balance wheel to draw the bobbin thread to the surface
Hold it together with the top thread and start with a few slow stitches.

Working steadily
Rest your forearms firmly on the machine table, spread fingers well out and well away from the needle. Move the frame around smoothly and slowly.

Using a sharp, new machine needle
A good first project to practise: try 'writing' your name on calico.

Machine embroidered calico curtains

A simple curtain with a 15 cm (6 in) band of free machine embroidery which has then been further embellished with lazy daisy (chain) stitch. In this case three pinks and two greens have been used. Measurements and colours could, of course, be easily varied to suit your own taste and colour scheme.

MATERIALS

Calico, 84 cm (33 in) square plus turnings, for main part of curtain; 51 cm × 41 cm (20 in × 16 in) plus turnings, for the yoked hanging loops

Sewing cottons in greens, pinks and cream

One hank of each of a range of pink and green DMC perlé, No 5

Crewel needle

Embroidery hoop

METHOD

1 Cut out the main area of calico, allowing generous turnings for any shrinkage during stretching.
2 Plan the design, either copying this one or designing your own.
3 Apply machine embroidery.
4 Further embellish the work with small irregular flowers in lazy daisy (chain) stitch using the perlé thread.
5 Stretch the work (see page 8).
6 Gather the embroidered end and reduce the width to 51 cm (20 in).
7 Turn the small side seams and the bottom hem.

To make the loops
1 Decide how many loops you need.
2 Trace our pattern and use it as a template, drawing lightly around the shape on to the calico, to denote the sewing line.
3 Repeat as many times as desired.
4 Cut out two identical areas, allowing 1.5 cm ($\frac{5}{8}$ in) for turnings, beyond the sewing line.
5 With RS of work together, sew the small side seams and then all the U shapes.
6 Trim the seams to 5 mm ($\frac{1}{4}$ in). Snip the curves and turn to RS. Press.

7 With RS together, place one of the long raw edges of this small yoke in line with the gathered edge of the embroidered section. Pin and tack together. Sew.
8 Fold each long tab and bring it down so that the raw edge is in line with the remaining unsewn raw edge of the yoke. Tack each one in position. Turn the 1.5 cm ($\frac{5}{8}$ in) seam allowance under and slip stitch both to the back of the gathered seam.

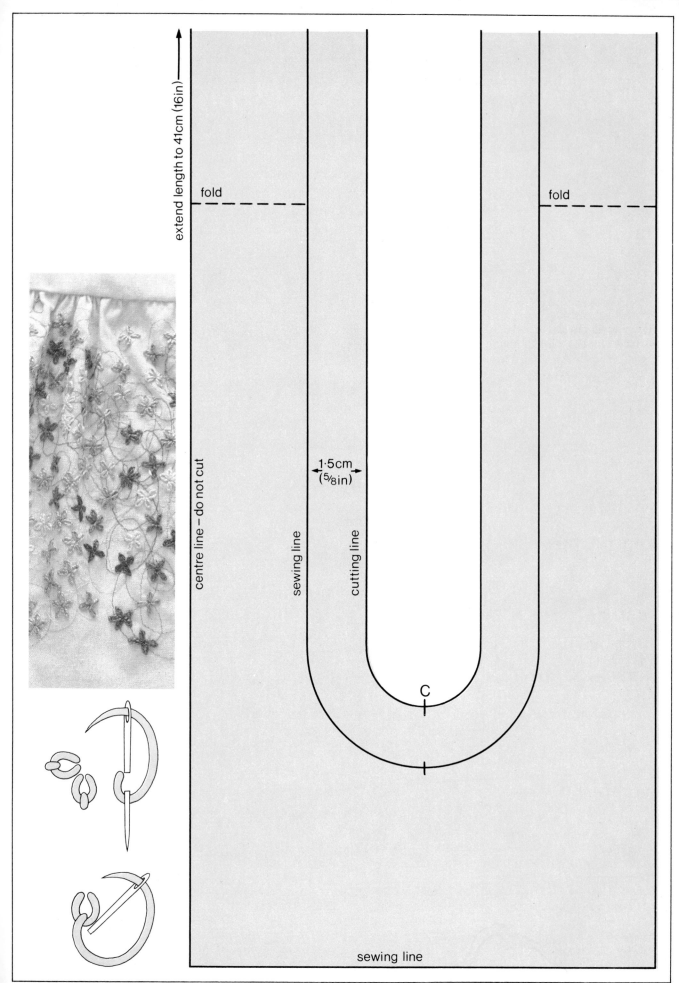

extend length to 41cm (16in)

fold

fold

centre line – do not cut

sewing line

cutting line

1·5cm
($^5/_8$in)

C

sewing line

Machine embroidered lampshade

*The delicate 'scrolly' effect of machine embroidery is particularly
well suited to a lampshade where the light will bring out the textures
of the thread. This small shade is made over a drum-shaped
wire frame obtainable from any large department store.*

This lampshade is quickly made. We
have used scraps of old plain white
embroidered ribbon and machine
embroidered them with some blue
'rainbow' embroidery cotton.
You will need a tacking foot and a
roll hemmer foot for the machine.
These are standard accessories for
most machines.

MATERIALS

Small drum shaped lampshade
frame.

Narrow tape to bind the frame

Vanishing muslin onto which other
fabrics or lace strips can be applied.
The size of the piece would have to
be the circumference of the frame ×
the height of the frame, plus 2.5 cm
(1 in) at least all round for turnings.

Threads One 25 g reel (880 yd) DMC
No 30 Retors D'Alsace (colour here
is 93)
One skein DMC perlé No 3 colour
796, for couching

Organdie for lining, a little smaller
than the size required for the
vanishing muslin

Sewing cotton for making up

Tacking foot and rollhemmer foot
for machine

METHOD

Note The multi-coloured rainbow
thread is used throughout.
1 Cut out a large enough area of
vanishing muslin (see above).
2 Tack strips of neutral embroidery
ribbon or lace to the ground area of
vanishing muslin. This muslin
totally supports the work so no
embroidery frame is necessary. The
foot of the machine is removed and
the teeth either lowered or covered
with a cover plate according to the
age of the sewing machine, in order

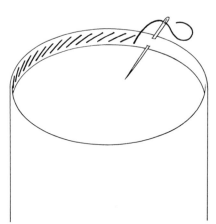

to achieve a straight free line. Apply
the strips of ribbon and decorate
with simple straight stitched lines.
3 The highly textured strips are
achieved by using the tacking foot
with only half the width of the needle
swing and a very close stitch length.
4 Couched lines have been achieved
by threading the perlé into the roll
hemmer and setting the machine to
a half width zigzag as above, but
allowing a little more space in the
stitch length.
5 When all the embroidery is complete, iron away the muslin with a
hot iron (making sure that the iron
is not on too hot a setting for the top
fabric). First the muslin turns brown
and then it crumbles away.
Alternatively, on a lampshade, it
does not spoil the effect to leave it in.
6 Bind the tape carefully around
every part of the wire frame. This
not only improves the final look of
the shade but gives a structure to
which it is much easier to attach
fabric.
7 Pin the embroidery around this
frame and sew it, with tiny overcast
stitches, to the top and bottom circle
of the frame, merely catching the
taped covering with the needle. Trim
after stitching, to 5 mm ($\frac{1}{4}$ in).
8 Fold under the turning allowed
for one side of the side seam and lap
over the other edge. Invisibly slip
stitch the length from top to bottom.
Repeat the process for the lining, but
this time turning in the top and
bottom edges, rather than folding
them over the frame.
9 Trim with a hand-made twisted
cord made in the remainder of the
perlé if so desired (see page 9). Slip
stitch it invisibly to the top and
bottom of the frame.

Machine embroidered tote bag

A small tote bag measuring 39 cm×48 cm (15 in×19 in). A double layer of felt achieves an almost quilted effect when held down with a single machine stitch line. Tonal contrast is then added by the removal of a few selected shapes from the upper layer.

MATERIALS

Felt Two layers of good quality felt in contrasting colours, not smaller than 53 cm × 42.5 cm (21 in × 16¾ in)

Two strips of the under colour felt 7.5 cm × 38 cm (3 in × 15 in), for the handles

Two strips 4.5 cm × 90 cm (1¾ in × 35½ in), for the sides

Two strips of heavy sew-in interfacing 2 cm × 38 cm (¾ in × 15 in)

No 3 piping cord: four lengths of 38 cm (15 in) and two lengths of 90 cm (35½ in)

Cutting out and embroidery scissors

No 1 paint brush and white poster paint

Sewing cotton for the machine embroidery and for making up (No 50, if possible)

Embroidery hoop

Strong tracing paper

Pencil

Crewel needle

French chalk, tailor's chalk or white pencil

METHOD

Preparing the design

1 With white chalk, mark out the total area needed for the bag, on the upper layer of felt. Also, carefully mark the stitching lines and seam allowances.

2 Trace the pattern supplied onto best quality tracing paper and transfer the design using the prick and pounce method (see page 7), pricking holes every 3 mm (⅛ in).

3 Move the tracing to the next area for pattern, making sure to link lines with the adjoining completed area.

4 When all the required pattern is

on the fabric, tack it to the second layer of felt.

Working the embroidery
1 Place the work in the hoop.
2 Remove the presser foot, cover the 'feed' and lower the lever. Select a narrow zigzag as instructed in your machine manual and work this over every painted line.
3 Select a number of shapes and using embroidery scissors carefully remove the top layer of felt to reveal a small amount of the colour of the second layer underneath.
4 Press carefully.

Making up the bag
Handles
1 Take the four lengths of piping cord 38 cm (15 in) long and the two strips of 7.5 cm × 38 cm (3 in × 15 in) felt in the under colour. Chalk a centre line lengthwise along both the strips.
2 Fold one edge of the strip over a length of piping cord and up to the chalk line. Stitch with zip foot close to the cord. Now fold in the other edge over a second length of cord, again to the chalk line. Stitch as before. Do this for both strips of felt. Now take the two 2 cm ($\frac{3}{4}$ in) wide interfacing strips and lay one for each handle between the two corded edges, allowing the two cut edges to come together and be joined with cretan stitch (see page 54).
3 Lay the handles in position on RS of the bag 7.5 cm (3 in) from the side seam line, with the raw edges in line with the top edge of the bag, and WS of the handle facing you. Tack.

Side seams and top
1 Take the two lengths of 90 cm ($35\frac{1}{2}$ in) piping cord and cover them with the 4.5 cm × 90 cm ($1\frac{3}{4}$ in × $35\frac{1}{2}$ in) felt strips in the under colour, using the machine zip foot to sew really close to the cord.
2 Working from the RS and with the bag still opened out flat, lay each length of prepared piped felt around the side seams and top of the bag, one piece travelling ABCD and the other EFGH (all raw edges should be in line). Pin, tack and sew with the zip foot attachment on the machine.
3 Carefully re-check both the cutting and sewing lines of bag. Fold the bag in half with RS of work together. Stitch the side seams with the zip foot.

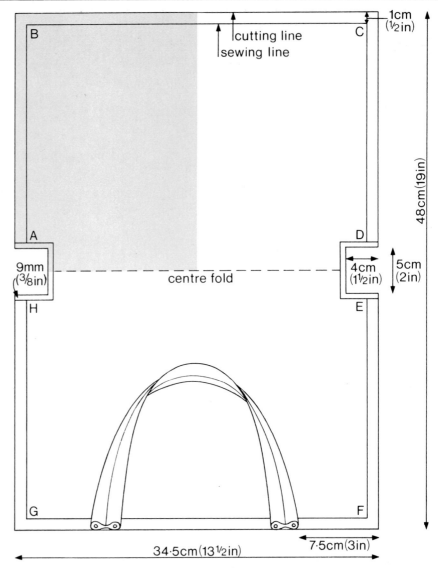

4 To form the width in the bottom of the bag: place RS together matching the side seam to the fold line. Stitch this open end with a 9 mm ($\frac{3}{8}$ in) seam.
5 Whilst at the inside top edge of bag, cut away the spare bulk of the turnings. leaving just the one layer of felt. Herringbone stitch this to the bag, making a neat inside top edge. (No stitches should go through to the right side).
6 Turn to RS. Reinforce the top of side seams, stitching right through from one side to the other. See page 12 for herringbone stitch.

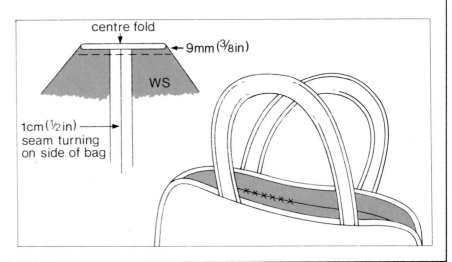

The pattern above fills exactly one-quarter of the material (shown by pink area on previous page).

Hanging wall-pocket

This useful 'wall-pocket' to hold cosmetics, is decorated with free machine embroidery inspired by sections of grapefruit. The 'segments' are cut away to reveal a pink layer underneath.

MATERIALS

A rectangular piece of orange sailcloth for the backing*

Another piece the same size for the lining

Three strips of orange sailcloth (the same width) for the pockets
Note The lowest set of pockets should be deeper than the rest

Strips the same size in pink poplin

Strips of pink or orange net

Strips of lightweight lining material for each row of pockets

Four strips 4 cm (1½ in) wide to bind raw edges

Tailor's chalk

Pencil

Tracing paper

*the size can be varied according to use. (You could embroider all the strips, or only one.)

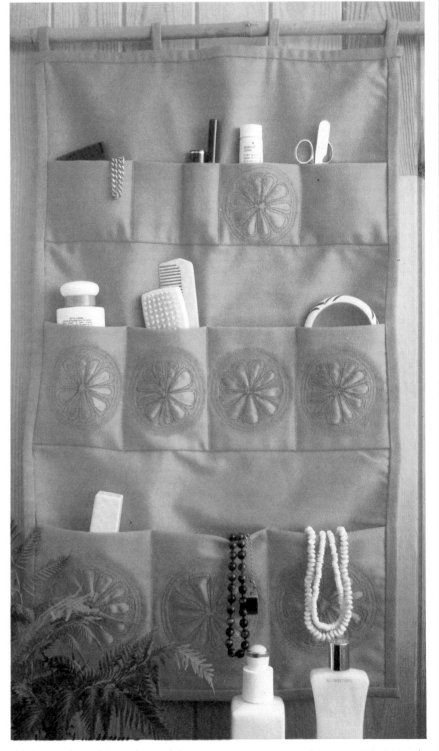

METHOD

Prepare the embroidered strip (or strips) first
1 Using tailor's chalk, draw vertical lines dividing the strip into three or four. These divisions will form the pockets.

2 Use a glass or small cup as a template and draw circles in the centre of each pocket.

3 Now, using sharp embroidery scissors, cut away each shape to leave circular holes. Cut the matching strip of pink fabric. Place this behind the holes RS pink to WS orange and tack the two layers together all round.

4 Use your cup or glass again, and draw round it, this time on tracing paper. Cut it out 1 cm ($\frac{1}{2}$ in) larger all round. Pin it to the layers of net and cut out, in double layers, however many circles you need.

5 Lay these net circles over the pink circles and tack them on securely all round the edge.

6 Prepare the machine for free machine embroidery and put the fabric in a hoop (see page 5). Now work the 'segments' in straight machine stitch around and across each circle over the net. Don't make them too even – look at half a real orange or grapefruit for inspiration if necessary! If you feel nervous about this stage, you could first draw the segment shapes on to tissue, tack it on, then machine over your drawn lines, gently tearing the tissue paper away later. Cut away the net in the segments.

Making up the wall pocket
Start with the bottom (deepest) pocket
1 To make a lining for each pocket: place the embroidered strip and lining RS together and machine the top edge. Turn to the RS and press. Trim away some of the turning to reduce bulk.

2 Put the bottom strip on top of the backing rectangle, RS together, and tack in place. Machine. Remove tackings. Press, and fold it up into position. It helps to fold up the seam allowance and press it before you attach it to the backing – the fold line acts as a guide for stitching. Now work two rows of straight or machine zigzag and then trim – this makes the inside of the pocket much neater. Tack the strip's sides in position, to hold in place during machining. Tack dividing lines between 'grapefruits'.

3 Now using a small, close zigzag (width 2, length 1) and matching thread, machine pocket lines. Start and finish with a reverse machine stitch for strength. Make the other strips and pockets in the same way. To keep them parallel, rule a line with tailor's chalk to mark the position of the upper pockets.

4 Place the lining WS to WS of the hanging. Tack it all round.

5 Bind the raw edges:
Measure the sides of the hanging and cut four strips the appropriate length 4 cm (1$\frac{1}{2}$ in) wide, allowing 2 cm ($\frac{3}{4}$ in) either end for turnings. Treat each side separately. Start with the two longer sides. Place the binding RS to RS raw edge of the hanging. Tack and machine 1 cm ($\frac{1}{2}$ in) from the edge. Remove the tackings. Press and fold over the raw edges. Turn under the raw edge of the binding, fold to the back and slip stitch neatly in place. Treat the other long side in the same way. Trim the binding edges level with the hanging.

6 Treat the two shorter sides in the same way, but fold in the remaining raw edges of the binding and slip stitch the folded edges neatly together.

7 Make hanging loops:
Cut four strips 4 cm × 12 cm (1$\frac{1}{2}$ in × 5 in). Fold lengthways RS together, and machine along one short end and down the length. Turn to the RS, using a knitting needle and press. Neaten the remaining raw edge with zigzag and trim. Fold in half and attach to the back of the hanging by strong hand stitches.

Where to study embroidery

The Embroiderers' Guild
Apartment 41A
Hampton Court Palace
East Moseley
Surrey

A small annual subscription gives varied privileges including access to a unique embroidery collection and library, and classes and activities at nominal prices. Lectures and classes in 71 branches spread all over Britain, are available for a small additional fee. *Send SAE for details.*

**Colleges offering
BA Hons Degree in Embroidery**

Birmingham College of Art and Design
New Corporation Street
Birmingham 4

Goldsmiths College
Millard Building
Cormont Road
Camberwell
London SE5

Loughborough College of Art
Radmoor
Loughborough

Manchester Polytechnic
Faculty of Art
All Saints
Manchester

Trent Polytechnic
School of Art and Design
Burton Street
Nottingham

Ulster College
Northern Ireland Polytechnic
Jordanstown
Newtonabbey
Co. Antrim

A similar qualification is obtainable in Scotland from:
Glasgow College of Art
167 Renfrew Street
Glasgow

There are numerous recreational classes held throughout the British Isles. Details of adult institutes can be obtained from local libraries and town halls.

Embroidery suppliers

This is a short list of suppliers who are willing to send by mail order. There are of course innumerable local shops who may already stock everything you need. A good source of further suppliers of materials and books is the magazine *Embroidery*. *Important* Enquire by post or phone first for price lists and catalogues, and please enclose a stamped and addressed envelope when writing.

de Denne Limited
159–161 Kenton Road
Kenton, Harrow
Middlesex
All DMC threads, embroidery books and 'Embroidery' magazine.

Ells and Farrier
5 Princes Street
Hanover Square
London W 1
Beads and Sequins

Felt and Hessian Shop
34 Greville Street
London EC1
Felt and Hessian

John Lewis
Oxford Street
London W1
(and similar, excellent large stores around the country)
Wadding, interfacing, every type of fabric, threads, wools, cottons, piping cords

MacCulloch and Wallis
25–26 Dering Street
London W1R 0BH
Rubber solution, fabric adhesive, Clarke's Anchor threads, Vanishing muslin, interfacing

Mace and Nairn
89 Crane Street
Salisbury
Wiltshire
All threads and wools, canvas

Nottingham Handicraft Limited
17 Ludlow Hill Road
Melton Road
West Bridgford
Nottingham NG2 6HD
Clarks Anchor threads, beads, felt, canvas, adhesives, interfacing, art materials

Christine Riley
53 Barclay Street
Stonehaven
Kincardineshire AB3 2AR
Clarks Anchor and DMC threads, canvas, hessian, felt, beads, Appletons wools

Silken Strands
33 Linksway
Gatley, Cheadle
Cheshire
Large selection of unusual threads including lurex and chenille

The Weavers Shop
Royal Wilton Carpet Factory
Wilton, Salisbury
Wiltshire SP2 0AY
Bags of mixed carpet thrums

Acknowledgments

The author would like to thank Linda Blakemore, the book designer and also the following who helped to make up the items:

Judith Abbott, Audrey Beaney, Barbara Birch, Mary Broughton, Kate Charles, Jane Clarke, Margaret Cooper, Jill Friend, Eileen Gregory, Joan Hardingham, Jackie Hill, Polly Hill, Joan Hake, Margaret Head, Hilda Ibrahim, Pauli Jennings, Judy March, Bridget Moss, Marjorie Minear, Phil Palmer, Joan Pestell, Linda Pestell, Valerie Riley, Edith Robinson, Mary Shea, Pat Wright, Dorothy Wooler.

Thanks are also due to the shops and manufacturers listed below for lending accessories:

Boots the Chemists for make-up and toiletries pages 34 and 78.
The Bedchamber for toys and pillow page 43 and crochet cover page 48.
W.M. Christy and Sons for bedlinen pages 41 and 50.
Dickins and Jones Limited for dress, blouse and skirt pages 38, 58, 59 and 69.
The Reject Shop for cane furniture pages 17 and 75, lamps pages 48 and 50, lamp base page 74 and and tray with china page 57.

Photographic stylist: Marie O'Hara